# REA
# STEADY
# COOK

BRIAN TURNER

ANTONY WORRALL
THOMPSON

PHOTOGRAPHS BY
JULIET PIDDINGTON

**BBC BOOKS**

This book is published to accompany the television series *Ready Steady Cook*
which was first broadcast in Autumn 1994.
The series is produced by Bazal Productions.

Published by BBC Books, an imprint of BBC Worldwide Publishing.
BBC Worldwide Ltd, Woodlands, 80 Wood Lane, London W12 0TT

First published 1996
Format © Bazal Productions
Recipes © Antony Worrall Thompson and Brian Turner
The moral right of the authors has been asserted
Editor: Jane Middleton
Home Economist: Carol Tennant
ISBN 0 563 38733 5

Set in Futura
Designed by Louise Morley
Printed by Martins the Printers Ltd., Berwick-upon-Tweed
Bound by Hunter & Foulis Ltd., Edinburgh
Colour Separations by Radstock Reproductions Ltd., Midsomer Norton
Colour printing by Lawrence Allen Ltd., Weston-super-Mare
Cover printed by Clays Ltd., St Ives Plc

# CONTENTS

# INTRODUCTION

At last! The *Ready Steady Cook* book has arrived. If you have ever started one of our recipes, fired with enthusiasm after the show, only to find you can't remember quite how it finished, this is the book for you.

On *Ready Steady Cook* we give our chefs the ultimate culinary test. The budget is £5, the time limit is 20 minutes and, on top of all that, the ingredients are a complete surprise. Our contestants have chosen a combination of foods they love and it's the chef's job to invent a delicious recipe there and then.

These recipes make it possible for anyone to rustle up a gourmet dish. The book is full of new ideas (even the chefs surprise themselves sometimes) and it's guaranteed to inspire good and bad cooks alike.

The point is to have a go – cooking is fun and the eating is even better! You can knock up a fabulous dish in 20 minutes for a fiver. Honestly. Go on – give it a try.

*Fern Britton*
x

Presenter, *Ready Steady Cook*

# A NOTE ON INGREDIENTS AND TECHNIQUES

Good-quality ingredients make all the difference to the taste of the finished dish. For best results, choose unsalted butter and extra virgin olive oil. Buy ripe, flavoursome tomatoes whenever possible and really fresh herbs. If a recipe specifies dried herbs, freeze-dried ones usually have the best flavour. For desserts, chocolate should contain at least 50 per cent cocoa solids – check the back of the packet.

> Some of the recipes contain raw or lightly cooked eggs. Because of the slight risk of salmonella poisoning, these should be avoided by the sick, the elderly, the very young, and pregnant women.
> The chances of contamination are greatly reduced if you buy free-range eggs, preferably organic, from a reputable supplier.

Many of the recipes in this book include wine. Use a wine that you would enjoy drinking rather than cheap 'cooking' wine – if it's not worth drinking, it's not worth cooking with!

Two techniques favoured by the chefs on *Ready Steady Cook* are cooking on a ridged grill pan and stock or sauce reduction.

Ridged grill pans are made of cast iron and usually have a spout for pouring off the cooking juices. They are a very healthy way of cooking because the ridges keep the food raised above any fat that runs off. They also make attractive grill marks on food – to make a crisscross pattern, give the food a half-turn half-way through cooking each side. Use ridged grill pans for steaks, chops, fish or chunky slices of vegetables such as aubergines, courgettes or peppers.

Stocks and sauces can be reduced by cooking them over a high heat until some of the liquid has evaporated. This concentrates the flavour and produces a thicker consistency. Because the flavour becomes more intense, you need to make sure you are using really good ingredients to start with – and in an ideal world this means homemade stock. However, you can buy fresh chilled stocks in cartons in supermarkets nowadays, which come a very good second best. In an emergency, take a tip from the chefs on *Ready Steady Cook* and use a stock cube diluted in a mixture of water and wine.

Finally, *Ready Steady Cook* is all about putting together a delicious meal from whatever ingredients you have to hand. The recipes in this book are proof that some of the most memorable dishes are the ones that come about on the spur of the moment. So if you don't have a particular ingredient, follow the example of our chefs and improvise. Don't be afraid to get in the kitchen and *Ready Steady Cook*!

# VEGETARIAN DISHES

## ANTONY WORRALL THOMPSON

# FUSILLI WITH AUBERGINE AND TOMATO SAUCE

*See photograph*

**SERVES 2**
225 g (8 oz) fusilli
5 tablespoons olive oil
1 small or 1/2 large aubergine, cut into slices
1 cm (1/2 inch) thick
1 garlic clove, chopped
1/2 teaspoon chilli powder, or to taste

225 g (8 oz) ripe plum tomatoes,
skinned and diced
2 teaspoons balsamic vinegar
1 tablespoon chopped fresh basil
Salt and freshly ground black pepper
A few sprigs of basil, to garnish

Cook the pasta in a large pan of boiling salted water for about 8 minutes or until *al dente*.

Meanwhile, make the sauce. Heat 3 tablespoons of the olive oil in a large frying pan and add the aubergine slices. Fry over a medium-high heat until tender and brown on both sides, then remove from the pan and drain on kitchen paper. When cool enough to handle, cut each slice into quarters. Heat 1 tablespoon of the remaining oil in the pan, add the garlic and chilli and cook gently for 1 minute without letting the garlic brown. Stir in the tomatoes, balsamic vinegar and chopped basil and season with salt and pepper to taste. Stir in the aubergines and remove from the heat.

To serve, drain the pasta and toss with the remaining olive oil, then mix with the aubergine and tomato sauce. Garnish with sprigs of basil.

---

### READY STEADY COOK Tip

*If you have time, it is a good idea to salt the aubergine slices first to remove any bitter juices. Place them in a colander, sprinkle with salt and leave to drain for 30 minutes to 1 hour, then rinse and pat dry.*

---

### ANTONY WORRALL THOMPSON

## PATRICIA'S FUNGHI TRICOLORI

Mushrooms stuffed with spinach and ricotta on a
tomato and herb sauce
*See photograph*

Patricia Roberts, a farmer's wife from Shrewsbury, had never cooked with ricotta cheese.
Antony showed her how, and used it to make a delicious stuffing for some giant mushrooms.

| | |
|---|---|
| **SERVES 2** | 3 tablespoons dry white wine |
| 4 large open-cap mushrooms | 1 x 400 g (14 oz) tin of chopped tomatoes |
| 40 g (1$\frac{1}{2}$ oz) butter | 1 tablespoon chopped fresh parsley |
| 3 garlic cloves, chopped | 1 tablespoon chopped fresh basil |
| 1 onion, finely chopped | 150 g (5 oz) Cheshire cheese, grated |
| 2 bay leaves | 225 g (8 oz) young spinach leaves |
| $\frac{1}{2}$ teaspoon dried oregano | 225 g (8 oz) ricotta cheese |
| $\frac{1}{2}$ teaspoon dried thyme | Salt and freshly ground black pepper |
| 1 teaspoon chopped fresh rosemary | A few basil leaves, to garnish |

Pre-heat the oven to gas mark 6, 200°C (400°F).

Peel the mushrooms and remove the stalks, then chop the stalks
finely and set aside. Divide 25 g (1 oz) of the butter between the
mushroom caps, season with salt and pepper and put in the oven for
5 minutes.

Heat the remaining butter in a frying pan, add the garlic, onion,
bay leaves, dried herbs and rosemary and cook gently for about 5
minutes, until the onion is softened. Remove half this mixture from the
pan and set aside. Add the chopped mushroom stalks, white wine
and tinned tomatoes to the pan and simmer for about 10 minutes,
until slightly thickened. Stir in the parsley and basil and cook for a
further 3–4 minutes, then add half the grated cheese and season with
pepper to taste.

Wash the spinach, discarding any large stalks, then place it in a pan with only the water clinging to the leaves and cook for about 2 minutes, until just wilted. Leave until cool enough to handle and then squeeze out as much liquid as you can. Blend the spinach, ricotta and reserved onion mixture in a food processor until smooth, then season to taste. Spoon into the mushroom caps and return them to the oven for 5–10 minutes to heat through.

Sprinkle with the remaining cheese and place under a hot grill until golden and bubbling.

To serve, pour the tomato and herb sauce on to 2 warmed serving plates, place the mushrooms on top and garnish with basil leaves.

ANTONY WORRALL THOMPSON

# A VARIATION ON VIV'S VARIOUS VEGETABLES
Deep-fried vegetables with rice patties and two dips

Vivien McManus from Cardiff is vegetarian and has varied tastes. Her father was in the army, which gave her the opportunity to travel the world, sampling local ingredients. She brought along a selection of vegetables with the addition of peanut butter, which she hoped would prove the ultimate challenge for Antony.

**SERVES 2–3**

1 large sweet potato, peeled and cut into thin chips
100 g (4 oz) okra, sliced into 1 cm ($1/2$ inch) lengths
1 cauliflower, cut into bite-sized florets
Sunflower oil for deep-frying
Salt and freshly ground black pepper
Sprigs of coriander, to garnish

**FOR THE RICE PATTIES**

100 g (4 oz) long grain rice
1 vegetable stock cube
1 lemon grass stalk, bruised
1 fresh kaffir lime leaf, or a strip of lime zest
$1/4$ fresh red chilli
1 tablespoon plain flour
1 egg, beaten
1 tablespoon sunflower oil
2 tablespoons smooth peanut butter

# VEGETARIAN DISHES

**FOR THE PEANUT DIP**
4 tablespoons smooth peanut butter
3 tablespoons double cream
2 teaspoons finely chopped onion
$3/4$ fresh red chilli, deseeded and finely chopped
Juice of $1/2$–1 lime, to taste
2 tablespoons chopped fresh coriander

**FOR THE YOGHURT DIP**
150 ml (5 fl oz) Greek yoghurt
2 teaspoons finely chopped onion
1 garlic clove, crushed
2 tablespoons chopped fresh mint

First cook the rice for the patties. Bring a pan of water to the boil, add the stock cube, lemon grass, kaffir lime leaf or lime zest and red chilli, then stir in the rice. Simmer for 10–12 minutes, until the rice is tender, then drain and leave to cool.

Next make the dips. Mix together all the ingredients for each one, adding seasoning to taste, then transfer to a small serving bowl and set aside. The peanut dip should be quite thick but if it is too stiff, stir in a little water.

Blanch the sweet potato chips in a pan of boiling water for 1 minute, then drain well and dry on kitchen paper.

Remove the lemon grass, lime and chilli from the cooled rice, then stir in the flour, beaten egg and seasoning to taste. Heat the oil in a large frying pan over a moderately high heat and spoon in the rice mixture in 6 portions. Flatten slightly with the back of the spoon, make a small indentation in the centre of each patty and spoon in 1 teaspoon of the peanut butter, covering it with a little of the rice from the edges. Cook for 5 minutes, turning once, until the patties are crisp and golden brown. Keep warm.

Heat the oil for deep-frying in a saucepan or deep-fryer and fry the okra, sweet potato chips and three quarters of the cauliflower florets. Cook them in separate batches for about 3 minutes each, until golden and tender, taking care not to overcrowd the pan. Drain on kitchen paper and sprinkle with salt.

To serve, arrange the deep-fried vegetables, rice patties and raw cauliflower on a serving platter and garnish with sprigs of coriander. Serve with the peanut and yoghurt dips.

## ANTONY WORRALL THOMPSON

# JACKIE'S ITALIAN STALLION

Bruschetta with olive paste, aubergine and Mozzarella
*See photograph*

Jackie Parrott from Hertfordshire is passionate about Italian food. She brought along her favourite ingredients and helped her favourite chef of all time cook this delicious recipe.

**SERVES 2**

4 tablespoons olive oil
2 large slices of white country-style bread, about 1 cm ($^1/_2$ inch) thick, crusts removed
1 garlic clove, cut in half
1 small or $^1/_2$ large aubergine, cut into slices 1 cm ($^1/_2$ inch) thick
1 x 100 g (4 oz) Mozzarella cheese in water (preferably buffalo Mozzarella), drained and sliced
Salt and freshly ground black pepper

**FOR THE OLIVE PASTE**

100 g (4 oz) black olives, pitted
1 garlic clove, chopped
$1^1/_2$ tablespoons olive oil
2 tablespoons chopped fresh coriander
$^1/_2$ teaspoon Dijon mustard
1 teaspoon balsamic vinegar

**TO GARNISH**

1 large, ripe, flavoursome tomato, sliced
A few basil leaves

First make the olive paste by blending all the ingredients in a food processor until smooth. Taste and season with salt and pepper.

To make the bruschetta, heat 1 tablespoon of the olive oil in a frying pan, add the bread and fry until golden. Remove from the pan and rub with the cut garlic clove. Heat the remaining oil in the pan and fry the aubergine slices over a medium-high heat until golden on both sides. Remove from the pan and drain on kitchen paper.

Spread some of the olive paste on to the bruschetta, cover with the aubergine slices and arrange the Mozzarella on top. Place under a hot grill until the cheese begins to melt.

To serve, place the bruschetta on 2 plates and garnish with the tomato and leaves. Drizzle with olive oil and grind over some pepper.

# FISH DISHES

FISH AND CHIPS À LA WARRINGTON – 16

FILLETS OF PLAICE EN VERDURE – 17

MOULES EN VAPEUR AVEC
TOMATES FARCIES – 19

JIMINY SALMON FINOCCHIO – 20

DEBBIE'S HOLLY POTATO, SALMON
AND OTHER THINGS – 22

JULIE'S JERSEY SALMON ROYALE – 24

ANDI'S SOLE WITH A HEART – 25

SPICY MACKEREL FILLETS
ON TASTY TENBY TREATS – 27

JADE AND AMBER'S FLAME SURPRISE – 29

## BRIAN TURNER

# FISH AND CHIPS À LA WARRINGTON

Battered cod with deep-fried potato balls and cabbage parcels

Karen Hawthorne from Warrington, Cheshire, hated fish – unless it came from a chippy. Brian converted her with a delicious dish of cod, prawns and potato balls

**SERVES 2**

2 x 150–175 g (4–6 oz) cod fillets, skinned
2 tablespoons plain flour, seasoned
1 small egg
2 tablespoons double cream
1 tablespoon chopped fresh parsley
3 tablespoons sunflower oil
Salt and freshly ground black pepper

**FOR THE CABBAGE PARCELS**
100 g (4 oz) frozen peas
1 sprig of mint

4–6 green cabbage leaves
50 g (2 oz) butter
200 g (7 oz) small peeled prawns
2 tomatoes, chopped
1 tablespoon chopped fresh parsley

**FOR THE POTATO BALLS**
350 g (12 oz) potatoes, grated
$1/2$ small onion, grated
4 tablespoons self-raising flour
Sunflower oil for deep-frying

Pre-heat the oven to gas mark 4, 180°C (350°F).

First prepare the cabbage parcels. Bring a large pan of water to the boil and add the peas and mint. Place the cabbage leaves on top and cook for 3–4 minutes, removing the cabbage leaves after 2 minutes. Drain the peas. Heat half the butter in a frying pan, add the prawns, tomatoes, peas and parsley and cook gently for 4–5 minutes. Season to taste, then drain well and spoon the mixture into the centre of each cabbage leaf. Gather each leaf up into a parcel, wrap it in a tea towel and give it a firm wring. Unwrap the tea towel and take out the stuffed cabbage leaf, which should remain in a neat parcel. Place the cabbage parcels in a greased ovenproof dish, dot with the remaining butter and bake in the oven for 8–10 minutes.

Meanwhile, make the potato balls. Mix together the potatoes, onion and flour, season and shape into 12–14 small balls. Heat the sunflower oil in a saucepan or deep-fat fryer, drop in the potato balls and fry for 3 minutes or until golden. Remove with a slotted spoon and drain on kitchen paper. Keep warm.

Dust the cod with the seasoned flour, shaking off any excess. Make a batter by whisking together the egg, cream, parsley and seasoning. Dip the fish in the batter. Heat the oil in a frying pan and fry the fish over a medium heat for 3–5 minutes on each side.

To serve, place the fish on 2 warmed serving plates and surround with the cabbage parcels and potato balls.

## B R I A N   T U R N E R

# FILLETS OF PLAICE EN VERDURE

Rolled plaice fillets with spinach moulds and herb butter sauce
*See photograph*

Jenny Evans from Manchester loves fish but hates the bones. She brought along some plaice, potatoes and spinach, which Brian transformed into her dream meal.

| | |
|---|---|
| **SERVES 2** | 1 large plaice, filleted and skinned |
| 100 g (4 oz) fresh spinach | 4 tablespoons dry white wine |
| 1 tablespoon olive oil | 400 ml (14 fl oz) fish or vegetable stock |
| 65 g (2½ oz) chilled butter | 3 tablespoons double cream |
| 1 small onion, finely diced | 2 tablespoons finely chopped fresh mixed |
| 2 garlic cloves, crushed | herbs, such as parsley, basil and tarragon |
| 1 large potato, finely diced | Salt and freshly ground black pepper |
| 3 tomatoes, skinned, de-seeded and chopped | |

Pre-heat the oven to gas mark 6, 200°C (400°F).

Wash the spinach, discarding any large stalks, then put it in a pan with only the water clinging to the leaves and cook for 2–3 minutes, until just wilted. Drain very thoroughly.

Heat the oil and 15 g ($^1/_2$ oz) of the butter in a frying pan and fry the onion, half the garlic and the potato for 10–15 minutes or until tender and golden brown. Add the tomatoes, reserving a few pieces for the sauce, and cook for 2 minutes. Season with salt and pepper to taste.

While the vegetables are cooking, place a spinach leaf on top of each plaice fillet, season, then roll up and fasten securely with a wooden cocktail stick. Place in a shallow casserole dish and pour over half the white wine and all except 3 tablespoons of the stock. Cook in the oven, uncovered, for about 5–6 minutes, until the fish is just done.

Meanwhile, line 2 greased 7.5 cm (3 inch) ramekin dishes or metal rings with the remaining spinach leaves, overlapping them and allowing the ends to overhang the edges of the containers. Fill with the tomato, onion and potato mixture, fold over the spinach to enclose the filling and bake in the oven for 10 minutes.

For the sauce, put the remaining wine and stock in a pan and boil until reduced to just under half its original volume. Add the remaining garlic and the reserved tomato pieces. Simmer for 2–3 minutes, then pass the sauce through a sieve into a clean pan and stir in the cream. Simmer for 3 minutes, then cut up the remaining butter and whisk it into the sauce a few pieces at a time until smooth. Stir in the chopped mixed herbs and season to taste.

To serve, place the fish rolls on 2 warmed serving plates and remove the cocktail sticks. Run a knife round the edge of the spinach moulds to loosen them and then turn them out and place next to the fish. Drizzle the sauce around the edges.

---

**READY STEADY COOK Tip**
*Ask your fishmonger to fillet and skin the plaice (there should be 4 fillets) and to give you the trimmings to make the stock.*

---

ANTONY WORRALL THOMPSON

# MOULES EN VAPEUR AVEC TOMATES FARCIES

Mussels steamed with coriander and lemon grass, served with stuffed tomatoes and lettuce chiffonade
*See photograph*

Ben Mills runs a sandwich shop in Bristol and his dream meal is musssels, beer and chips. Antony obliged with a magnificent moules dish.

**SERVES 2**
900 g (2 lb) mussels
1 Little Gem lettuce
40 g (1½ oz) butter
1 small onion, finely diced
2 garlic cloves, chopped
2 tablespoons chopped fresh coriander leaves
1 lemon grass stalk, finely chopped
½ teaspoon dried thyme
A pinch of chilli powder

120 ml (4 fl oz) dry white wine
salt and freshly ground black pepper

**FOR THE TOMATOES**
100 g (4 oz) fresh goat's cheese
½ small onion, very finely diced
3 anchovy fillets, chopped
1 tablespoon chopped fresh parsley
4 large tomatoes
15 g (½ oz) butter

Clean the mussels by scrubbing them thoroughly under cold running water and removing the beards. Cut the stalk out of the lettuce, reserve a few outer leaves and slice the rest into chiffonade (very fine strips).

For the tomatoes, mash together the goat's cheese, onion, anchovies and parsley, then season to taste. Slice the tops off the tomatoes and carefully scoop out the insides. Stuff with the goat's cheese mixture, put a knob of the butter on top of each one and place under a hot grill for 4–5 minutes, until heated through and lightly browned on top.

Meanwhile, cook the mussels. Melt 25 g (1 oz) of the butter in a pan, add the onion and garlic and cook gently for a few minutes until softened but not coloured. Stir in the coriander, lemon grass, thyme, chilli and wine, bring to the boil, then add the mussels. Cover and cook over a fairly high heat for 2–3 minutes, shaking the pan occasionally, until the shells have opened. Strain the mussels through a colander, reserving the liquid. Discard any mussels that remain closed. Pour the liquid into a pan and add the remaining butter. Simmer for a few minutes until slightly reduced, then stir in most of the lettuce chiffonade. Taste and adjust the seasoning.

To serve, open up the mussels and discard the top half of the shell, then arrange them around the edges of 2 heated serving plates. Place the reserved whole lettuce leaves in the centre and put the stuffed tomatoes on top, then pour the sauce over the mussels. Scatter over the remaining lettuce.

## ANTONY WORRALL THOMPSON

# JIMINY SALMON FINOCCHIO

Poached salmon with fennel, scallops, rice and watercress sauce

*Jackie Orr from North London adores fish. She presented Antony with a luxurious selection of ingredients and he created this superb dish for her.*

**SERVES 2**

100 g (4 oz) basmati rice

1 fennel bulb, cut into 6–8 wedges

450 ml (15 fl oz) vegetable stock

75 g (3 oz) watercress, leaves and stalks separated

2 x 175 g (6 oz) salmon steaks

40 g ($1\frac{1}{2}$ oz) butter

2 shallots, finely chopped

4 tablespoons dry white wine

1 small garlic clove, chopped

1 teaspoon chopped fresh thyme

1 bay leaf

150 ml (5 fl oz) double cream

A good squeeze of lemon juice

2 tablespoons olive oil

6 spring onions, chopped into 1 cm ($\frac{1}{2}$ inch) lengths

100 g (4 oz) scallops

1 teaspoon balsamic vinegar

Salt and freshly ground black pepper

Cook the rice in boiling salted water for 10–12 minutes, until just tender, then drain and keep warm. Cook the fennel in boiling salted water for about 6 minutes, until almost tender, then drain and set aside.

Pour the stock into a pan, add the watercress stalks and heat almost to boiling point. Season the salmon steaks and poach them in the stock for about 7 minutes, until just cooked. Remove from the pan, peel off the skin and keep the fish warm in a low oven. Leave the pan containing the stock on the heat and boil until reduced to a third of its original volume, then strain.

To make the sauce, melt 25 g (1 oz) of the butter in a small pan, add the shallots and sweat until softened. Add the white wine, garlic, thyme, bay leaf and reduced stock and simmer until the liquid has reduced to a third of its original volume. Stir in the cream and a good handful of the watercress leaves, then purée in a liquidizer until smooth. Return to the heat, add the lemon juice and simmer gently for 1–2 minutes. Taste and adjust the seasoning if necessary.

Heat the remaining butter and half the oil in a pan, add the spring onions and fennel and cook briskly for 5 minutes, until browned. Slice each scallop into 2 or 3 pieces, add to the pan and cook for between 30 seconds and 1 minute.

Mix together the balsamic vinegar, remaining olive oil and some salt to make a dressing. Pour on to the remaining watercress and toss well.

To serve, arrange the watercress salad on 2 warmed serving plates and place the salmon steaks on top. Spoon the rice to one side of the fish and the fennel and scallop mixture to the other. Pour the sauce around the edge.

---

### READY STEADY COOK Tip
*Be careful not to overcook the scallops or they will be tough. They are done when opaque but slightly translucent in the centre.*

---

## BRIAN TURNER

# DEBBIE'S HOLLY POTATO, SALMON AND OTHER THINGS

Salmon and smoked trout parcels with potato pancakes, brandy cream sauce and watercress and orange salad

Deborah Barker's husband hates fish but she and her children love it. Brian created the ultimate treat, and Debbie contributed a festive decoration.

### SERVES 2

75 g (3 oz) full-fat soft cheese
2 teaspoons yoghurt
1 tablespoon finely snipped fresh chives
175 g (6 oz) fresh salmon fillet, skinned and cut crosswise into 2.5 cm (1 inch) strips
100 g (4 oz) smoked trout fillet, cut lengthwise into 2.5 cm (1 inch) strips
150 ml (5 fl oz) fish or vegetable stock
4 tablespoons dry white wine
5 tablespoons double cream
A dash of brandy
50 g (2 oz) chilled butter, diced
2 tablespoons chopped mixed fresh herbs
Salt and freshly ground black pepper

### FOR THE POTATO PANCAKES

275 g (10 oz) potatoes, diced
50 g (2 oz) plain flour
A pinch of salt
1 egg
120 ml (4 fl oz) milk
1 tablespoon olive oil

### FOR THE SALAD

1 orange, peeled and divided into segments
1 bunch of watercress
2 tablespoons olive oil
2 teaspoons fresh orange juice

Pre-heat the oven to gas mark 6, 200°C (400°F).

To make the fish parcels, mix together the cream cheese, yoghurt and chives and season with salt and pepper. Lay each strip of salmon across the centre of a strip of smoked trout, spoon a little of the cream cheese mixture on top and fold the trout over to form a parcel. Place the fish parcels in a buttered shallow ovenproof dish. Put the stock and half the wine in a pan and bring to the boil, then pour it around the fish (it should come no more than half-way up the sides of the parcels). Cover with foil and bake in the oven for 8 minutes. Remove the fish parcels from the dish and keep warm; reserve the cooking liquid.

To make the pancakes, cook the potatoes in boiling salted water until tender, then drain and mash. Leave to cool. Whisk together the flour, salt, egg and milk, then add the mashed potato and whisk thoroughly until smooth. Heat the oil in a heavy-based frying pan. Pour in a couple of tablespoons of batter for each pancake and cook for about 3 minutes on each side or until golden brown. Keep warm.

For the sauce, put the remaining white wine in a pan and boil until reduced to about 1 tablespoon. Stir in the cream and brandy and simmer until reduced by half, then stir in 3 tablespoons of the reserved fish cooking liquid. Simmer until slightly reduced, then whisk in the butter a few pieces at a time until smooth. Stir in the mixed herbs and season to taste.

For the salad, arrange the orange segments on a bed of the watercress. Whisk together the oil and orange juice, season to taste and pour over the salad.

To serve, put the potato pancakes on 2 warmed serving plates and place the salmon and trout parcels on top. Pour the sauce over and accompany with the salad.

---

### READY STEADY COOK Tip
*If it's Christmas, why not try making Debbie's holly potato garnish? Peel a large potato and cut it into slices about 5 mm (¼ inch) thick. Cut them into holly shapes and fry in a little olive oil until crisp and golden.*

## B R I A N   T U R N E R

# JULIE'S JERSEY SALMON ROYALE

Salmon with lemon butter, courgette ribbons and two salads

Julie Witt and her identical twin Jayne travelled from Jersey to challenge one another on *Ready Steady Cook*. Julie brought Brian some salmon and homegrown Jersey potatoes.

**SERVES 2**
2 small eggs, hard-boiled
3 tablespoons chopped fresh parsley
2 x 150–175 g (5–6 oz) salmon fillets, skinned
50 g (2 oz) butter
Juice of ¹/₂ lemon
Salt and freshly ground black pepper

**FOR THE WARM POTATO SALAD**
225 g (8 oz) small new potatoes, preferably Jersey Royals
150 ml (5 fl oz) chicken stock
1 teaspoon grainy mustard
2 tablespoons mayonnaise

**FOR THE COURGETTE RIBBONS**
1 tablespoon olive oil
15 g (¹/₂ oz) butter
2 courgettes, sliced into ribbons with a vegetable peeler

**FOR THE MIXED SALAD**
3 tablespoons olive oil
1 tablespoon white wine vinegar
3 tomatoes, quartered
1 cucumber, diced
4 spring onions, sliced
A few lettuce leaves

First make the potato salad. Cook the potatoes in boiling salted water until tender, then drain. Pour the stock into a pan and boil until reduced to about 1 tablespoon. Stir in the mustard and mayonnaise and toss the potatoes in this dressing while still hot.

Push the hard-boiled eggs through a sieve, mix with the parsley and season well with salt and pepper. Coat one side of each salmon fillet (not the skin side) with this mixture, pressing it on firmly with your hands. Melt half the butter in a frying pan and fry the salmon, coated-side down, for 3 minutes. Turn and cook for another 3 minutes.

# FISH DISHES

For the courgette ribbons, heat the olive oil and butter in a large frying pan, add the courgettes and toss over a medium heat for about 2 minutes, until just tender. Season to taste.

For the mixed salad, whisk together the olive oil and vinegar and season to taste. Arrange the tomatoes, cucumber and spring onions on a bed of lettuce leaves, pour over the dressing and toss lightly.

To serve, melt the remaining butter in a frying pan until just starting to sizzle, then remove from the heat and stir in the lemon juice. Put the courgette ribbons on 2 warmed serving plates and arrange the salmon fillets on top. Pour the lemon butter over the fish and serve the salads separately.

## ANTONY WORRALL THOMPSON

# ANDI'S SOLE WITH A HEART
### Lemon sole with red pepper sauce, braised chicory, potatoes and guacamole

Andi Theobald from Kettering, Northamptonshire, had just returned from a three-month trip to India and was pleased to get back to some home cooking! As an ex-dancer, she's keen on healthy eating and brought Antony a lemon sole in the hope of increasing her fish repertoire.

**SERVES 2**
3 large potatoes
25 g (1 oz) butter
12 basil leaves
4 lemon sole fillets
1 tablespoon olive oil
Sunflower oil for deep-frying
Salt and freshly ground black pepper

**FOR THE GUACAMOLE**
1 avocado
1 tomato, finely chopped

2 tablespoons chopped fresh coriander
A pinch of chilli powder or cayenne pepper
1/4 red onion, finely chopped
Lime or lemon juice, to taste

**FOR THE CHICORY**
1 tablespoon olive oil
2 heads of chicory, sliced
A squeeze of lemon juice

**FOR THE RED PEPPER SAUCE**
1 red pepper, quartered and de-seeded
3 tablespoons double cream

25

Pre-heat the oven to gas mark 6, 200°C (400°F).

First make the guacamole. Peel and stone the avocado, then mash it with a fork. Stir in the remaining ingredients and season to taste with salt and pepper. Cover and set aside.

For the chicory, heat the olive oil in a small pan, then add the chicory and some salt and pepper. Cook for about 2 minutes, turning the chicory occasionally, then add the lemon juice, cover and cook for about 15 minutes, until very tender.

For the red pepper sauce, place the pepper quarters under a hot grill until charred and blistered. When cool enough to handle, peel off the skin and purée the pepper in a food processor or liquidizer. Add the cream and continue to process until smooth. Pour into a small pan, season to taste and reheat gently.

Peel and dice 2 of the potatoes and cook them in boiling salted water until tender. Drain and mash with the butter and seasoning to taste. Keep warm.

Lay 3 basil leaves on each lemon sole fillet, season and then roll up the fish with the basil leaves in the centre. Heat the olive oil in a shallow casserole dish or a small ovenproof frying pan and gently fry the fish on all sides for 2 minutes. Cover with a lid or aluminium foil and place in the oven for about 5 minutes to finish cooking.

Heat the oil for deep-frying in a saucepan or deep-fat fryer. Peel the remaining potato, then slice it as thinly as possible, using a vegetable peeler, a mandolin slicer or a very sharp knife. Pat the slices dry and then fry for 2–3 minutes, until golden brown. Drain the potato crisps on kitchen paper and sprinkle with salt.

To serve, pipe or spoon the mashed potato into the centre of a warmed serving platter. Remove the fish fillets from the pan with a fish slice to drain off the cooking juices and arrange them around the potato with the chicory. Pour the red pepper sauce over the fish and scatter over the potato crisps. Serve the guacamole separately.

---

### READY STEADY COOK Tip
*You could serve the guacamole as a starter with tortilla chips.*

---

## B R I A N   T U R N E R

# SPICY MACKEREL FILLETS ON TASTY TENBY TREATS

*See photograph*

Trevayne Keohane from Tenby, West Wales, needed new ideas for cooking mackerel, as her nephew, a keen fisherman, often dumps them on her doorstep. Brian obliged with a delicious recipe using spinach and apple to complement the flavour of the fish.

**SERVES 4**

1 small loaf of white bread, preferably slightly stale
65 g (2$^1/_2$ oz) butter
1 tablespoon olive oil
2 tablespoons plain flour
$^1/_2$ teaspoon paprika
$^1/_2$ teaspoon cayenne pepper
$^1/_2$ teaspoon ground cumin
$^1/_2$ teaspoon garam masala
4 mackerel fillets
1 tablespoon chopped fresh parsley
Salt and freshly ground black pepper

**FOR THE APPLE AND SPINACH MIXTURE**

1 tablespoon olive oil
15 g ($^1/_2$ oz) butter
1 onion, diced
1 large cooking apple, peeled, cored and diced
175 g (6 oz) fresh spinach

**FOR THE PATTYPAN SQUASH MIXTURE**

1 tablespoon olive oil
175 g (6 oz) pattypan squash, diced
3 garlic cloves, crushed
4 tomatoes, cut into wedges

Pre-heat the oven to gas mark 6, 200°C (400°F).

Cut the loaf of bread horizontally in half and carefully cut out the centre from each half, leaving a thin shell. Cut half the bread into 2 cm ($^3/_4$ inch) cubes (you don't need the rest of the soft bread for this recipe but you could make it into breadcrumbs for use in another dish; freeze them until required). Melt 25 g (1 oz) of the butter and brush it over the inside of the bread shells, then bake them in the oven for 6–8 minutes, until golden brown and crisp.

Heat the olive oil and 15 g ($^1/_2$ oz) of the remaining butter in a large frying pan and fry the bread cubes for about 4 minutes, until crunchy and golden brown. Set aside.

For the apple and spinach mixture, heat the oil and butter in a large pan, add the onion and cook gently for 5 minutes. Stir in the apple and cook for 5 minutes longer, until the apple is soft but still holds its shape.

Meanwhile, wash the spinach well, discarding any large stalks. Place in a large pan with just the water clinging to the leaves and cook for 3–4 minutes, until wilted.

Drain off any excess liquid and stir the spinach into the apple and onion mixture. Season to taste.

For the pattypan mixture, heat the oil in a pan and fry the squash for 5 minutes. Add the garlic and tomatoes, season and cook gently for about 5 minutes, until the squash is tender.

Next prepare the fish. Mix together the flour and spices. Coat the mackerel fillets with this mixture, shaking off any excess. Heat the remaining butter in a large frying pan and fry the fish over a medium-high heat for 2–3 minutes per side, until crisp on the outside and firm to the touch.

To serve, put the bread shells on a large serving plate, spoon the apple and spinach mixture into them and garnish with the croutons. Arrange the pattypan squash mixture around the bread shells and place the mackerel fillets on top. Sprinkle over the chopped parsley.

---

### READY STEADY COOK Tips
- *Pattypan squash are now stocked by most supermarkets in the summer months. They are members of the same family as courgettes. So if you cannot find them, you could substitute small, firm courgettes.*
- *If you are very short of time you could make this recipe without the bread, just serving the spicy fried mackerel with the two vegetable mixtures.*

## ANTONY WORRALL THOMPSON

# JADE AND AMBER'S FLAME SURPRISE

Trout with ginger and garlic on a bed of oriental noodles with a crispy carrot and leek garnish

Margaret Roberts, a registrar of births from Harlow, Essex, told Fern that Jade, Amber and Scarlett – 'a nice set of traffic lights' – were popular new names. Meanwhile Antony cooked up a colourful and delicious dish – and nearly set the studio on fire.

**SERVES 2**

2 x 175–225 g (6–8 oz) trout, gutted and trimmed
6 thin slices of fresh root ginger
2 garlic cloves, finely chopped
1 tablespoon plain flour
$\frac{1}{2}$–1 teaspoon chilli powder, to taste
3 tablespoons olive oil

**FOR THE NOODLES**

4 spring onions
1 vegetable stock cube
3 thin slices of fresh root ginger and
1 teaspoon finely grated ginger

175 g (6 oz) Chinese egg noodles
1 tablespoon vegetable oil
1 garlic clove, finely chopped
1 teaspoon chilli powder
2 tablespoons soy sauce
2 tablespoons dry white wine (optional)
1–2 tablespoons chopped fresh coriander

**FOR THE GARNISH**

Sunflower oil for deep-frying
2 carrots, cut into fine matchsticks
1 leek, cut into fine matchsticks
A few sprigs of coriander

Score the trout on both sides with a sharp knife, then put the ginger slices and garlic in the body cavities. Mix the flour and chilli powder together and sprinkle over the fish. Heat the olive oil in a large frying pan and fry the trout for 5 minutes on each side or until just cooked through. Remove from the heat and keep warm.

While the trout are cooking, prepare the noodles. Finely chop the white parts of the spring onions and set aside; reserve the green tops.

Crumble the stock cube into a pan of water and add the green spring onion tops and the ginger slices. Bring to the boil, then add the noodles and cook for 3 minutes or until just tender. Drain thoroughly and remove the spring onions and ginger slices. Heat the vegetable oil in a pan, add the garlic, grated ginger, chilli and chopped spring onions and cook for 1 minute. Stir in the noodles, soy sauce and wine, if using, and toss until heated through. Stir in the coriander and keep warm.

For the garnish, heat the sunflower oil in a saucepan or deep-fat fryer and deep-fry first the carrots and then the leeks for 2–3 minutes, until they are brown and crispy. Drain on kitchen paper.

To serve, arrange the noodles on 2 warmed serving plates and place the trout on top. Put the carrots and leeks in 2 neat piles on top of the fish and garnish with the sprigs of coriander.

---

### READY STEADY COOK Tip
*The easiest way to cut the carrots into fine matchsticks, or julienne, is to slice them into ribbons with a vegetable peeler, stack up the ribbons, then cut them in half across the centre and slice lengthwise into very fine strips.*

---

# POULTRY AND GAME

CHICKEN PRINCIPALITY – 32

THE CHATTANOOGA CHOO CHOO – 33

POULET SAUTÉ À LA MARMELADE DE JAN – 35

SPINACH-STUFFED CHICKEN LEG ON
TURMERIC-BRAISED POTATOES WITH
CUMIN-FRIED ONIONS – 36

ATLANTA CHICKEN WITH KUMQUAT CHUTNEY
AND ASPARAGUS – 38

BERTIE'S BUDGET VIRGIN CHICKEN WITH A
LITTLE SUMMER SOUP – 40

DANISH-STYLE PHEASANT WITH YORKSHIRE
BUBBLE AND SQUEAK – 42

MITCH'S BI-FOCAL CHICKEN – 43

POULET FARCI LOUISE BLANDFORD – 45

J. J.'S MAURITIAN FANCY – 47

HONEY AND LIME CHICKEN WITH ROASTED
CELERIAC, CHICKEN LIVER MOUSSE AND
MUSHROOM SAUCE – 49

STUFFED TURKEY STEAKS WITH BEAN STEW AND
DINO PASTA – 51

## BRIAN TURNER

# CHICKEN PRINCIPALITY

Stuffed chicken breasts with mixed vegetables and mead sauce

Sue Hindle from Falmouth enjoys entertaining. She gave Brian some Cornish mead and he showed her how to make a fabulous dish for her next dinner party.

**SERVES 2**
2 eggs, hard-boiled
2 tablespoons finely chopped black olives
15 g ($^1/_2$ oz) butter
3 tomatoes, cut in half
2 baby cauliflowers
100 g (4 oz) green beans
Salt and freshly ground black pepper

**FOR THE CHICKEN**
2 boneless skinless chicken breasts
65 g ($2^1/_2$ oz) butter

1 tablespoon chopped fresh parsley
1 tablespoon plain flour
1 egg, lightly beaten
$^1/_2$ tablespoon double cream
1 tablespoon olive oil

**FOR THE SAUCE**
120 ml (4 fl oz) Cornish mead or red wine
300 ml (10 fl oz) chicken stock
3 sprigs of rosemary
1 tablespoon balsamic vinegar

Pre-heat the oven to gas mark 6, 200°C (400°F).

Slit each chicken breast lengthwise down the centre, being careful not to cut all the way through. Use the knife to fold back the flesh and form a pocket, then flatten slightly with the palms of your hands. Season generously with salt and pepper, then put 25 g (1 oz) of the butter and $^1/_2$ tablespoon of chopped parsley on each breast. Roll up and coat in the flour. Lightly whisk together the egg and cream and dip the chicken breasts in this mixture. Heat the olive oil and remaining butter in a frying pan, add the chicken and fry for 3 minutes on each side. Transfer to the oven for about 5 minutes to complete the cooking.

Remove the yolks from the hard-boiled eggs and discard (or save to

Above: Potiron à la Flamande (page 74).
Below: Jackie's Italian Stallion (page 14) and Fusilli with Aubergine

Above: Spicy Mackerel Fillets on Tasty Tenby Treats (page 27).
Below: Lynn's Steak of Many Colours (page 67).

Above: Atlanta Chicken with Kumquat Chutney
and Asparagus (page 38).
Below: Fruit Hearts (page 89) and Chocolate Mousse (page 83).

Above: Patricia's Funghi Tricolori (page 11).
Below: Pears with Cranberry Compote and
Two-Chocolate Sauce (page 90).

Above: Baked Bananas with Pineapple Carpaccio and
Caramel Sauce (page 87).
Below: Poulet Farci Louise Blandford (page 45).

Above: Fillet of Pork Tout le Monde (page 71).
Below: Black Pudding à la Forestière with
Piedmontese Peppers (page 73).

Above: Fillets of Plaice en Verdure (page 17).
Below: Spaghetti Bolognese Black Watch Beetle (page 70)
and Farfalle Carbonara (page 72).

Above: The Humber Bridge Vegetable Hotpot (page 65).
Below: Moules en Vapeur avec Tomates Farcies (page 19).

use in sandwiches or salads). Push the egg whites through a sieve and mix with the chopped olives. Melt the butter in a pan, then remove from the heat and stir in the olive mixture.

Season the tomato halves and heat through under a hot grill, cut-side up. Cook the baby cauliflowers and green beans in boiling salted water for about 4 minutes, until just tender, then drain. Keep warm.

To make the sauce, put the mead or red wine, stock and rosemary in a pan and boil until reduced by half. Stir in the balsamic vinegar and simmer for 3 minutes, until the sauce has thickened slightly.

To serve, place each chicken breast in the centre of a warmed serving plate and put the cauliflowers and beans to the side. Place the tomatoes around the edge and pour the sauce over the chicken. Spoon the egg and olive mixture over the chicken and vegetables.

A N T O N Y   W O R R A L L   T H O M P S O N

# THE CHATTANOOGA CHOO CHOO

Spicy chicken with saffron rice, seafood and stuffed tomatoes

Michelle Atkinson's paella was always a disaster. Antony adapted the traditional Spanish dish and named it after her home next to a railway line in Northallerton, Yorkshire.

| SERVES 2 | 2 tablespoons olive oil |
|---|---|
| 450 g (1 lb) mussels | 4 tomatoes |
| 175 g (6 oz) basmati rice | 100 g (4 oz) frozen peas |
| 2 good pinches of saffron | 1 onion, finely chopped |
| 75 g (3 oz) butter | 200 ml (7 fl oz) double cream |
| 1 teaspoon dried thyme | 8 large cooked tiger prawns, heads |
| 150 ml (5 fl oz) dry white wine | removed but tails left on |
| 2 chicken drumsticks | 1 tablespoon pitted black olives, halved |
| 1/2 teaspoon cayenne pepper | Salt and freshly ground black pepper |

Pre-heat the oven to gas mark 6, 200°C (400°F).

Clean the mussels by scrubbing them thoroughly under cold running water and removing the beards.

Cook the rice in boiling salted water with 1 pinch of saffron for 10–12 minutes, until just tender, then drain.

Heat 25 g (1 oz) of the butter in a large pan with the thyme and white wine. Add the mussels, cover and cook over a fairly high heat for 2–3 minutes, until the shells have opened, shaking the pan occasionally. Drain, reserving the juices, and discard any mussels that remain closed.

Season the chicken drumsticks with the cayenne. Heat the olive oil in a frying pan and brown the chicken for 5 minutes on each side. Transfer to the oven and roast for 15–20 minutes, until cooked through.

Skin and quarter 2 of the tomatoes and set aside. Cut the other 2 in half and scoop out the seeds.

Cook the peas in boiling salted water for about 3 minutes, then drain. Fry the onion in the remaining butter until soft, then add the peas. Stir in 1 tablespoon of the reserved mussel juices. Fill the tomato halves with a little of this mixture and heat through under a hot grill or in the oven. Add the rice to the remaining onion and peas, season with salt and pepper and stir the mixture thoroughly.

Pour the remaining mussel juice into a separate pan, add the remaining saffron and boil until the liquid is reduced to half its original volume. Stir in the cream and cook gently for about 5 minutes. Season to taste.

To serve, spoon the rice on to 2 warmed serving plates. Place the chicken and stuffed tomatoes in the centre and pour the sauce over the top. Garnish with the mussels, reserved tomato quarters, tiger prawns and olives.

---

### READY STEADY COOK Tip
*When you are cleaning the mussels, if any of them have open shells, tap them firmly with your fingers. The shell should close at once; if not, it means the mussel is dead and should be thrown away.*

---

## BRIAN TURNER

# POULET SAUTÉ À LA MARMELADE DE JAN

### Fried chicken with marmalade sauce

Jan Perry from Telford, Shropshire, brought a whole chicken and some home-made marmalade – plus a bottle of tranquillizers in case Brian got into a pickle. Brian kept his cool and cooked a sumptuous meal.

| SERVES 3–4 | FOR THE SAUCE |
|---|---|
| 350 g (12 oz) small courgettes, grated | 2 tablespoons orange marmalade |
| 3 tablespoons olive oil | 4 tablespoons dry white wine |
| 75 g (3 oz) butter | 300 ml (10 fl oz) chicken stock |
| 1 x 1.25 kg (2 lb 12 oz) chicken, cut into 8 pieces | 50 g (2 oz) butter |
| 1 red and 1 yellow pepper | 1 tablespoon chopped fresh parsley |
| 1 onion, grated | 1 tablespoon chopped fresh dill |
| Salt and freshly ground black pepper | |

Place the grated courgettes in a sieve, sprinkle with salt and leave to drain while you cook the chicken. Heat 2 tablespoons of the oil and 50 g (2 oz) of the butter in a large shallow pan. Season the chicken pieces, then add to the pan, skin-side down, and brown on all sides. Cover and cook for 20–25 minutes, until tender. Remove the chicken and keep warm. Reserve the juices in the pan.

Cut the red and yellow peppers in half and remove the seeds. Finely chop half the red and half the yellow pepper and set aside. Cut each remaining pepper half into 3 strips. Heat the remaining oil in a ridged grill pan or a frying pan and fry the pepper strips for about 3 minutes on each side. Sprinkle with salt and set aside.

35

Rinse and drain the courgettes, pat dry. Heat the remaining butter in a pan and fry the diced pepper for 3 minutes. Add the courgettes and onion, season and cook for a further 3 minutes, until softened.

For the sauce, gently warm the marmalade, then sieve it to remove the peel. Pour the wine into the pan in which the chicken was cooked and bring to the boil, stirring well to scrape up the sediment from the base of the pan. Add the stock, marmalade, butter, parsley and dill and boil rapidly for 3–4 minutes, until reduced to about half its original volume. Taste and adjust the seasoning if necessary.

To serve, spoon the courgette and pepper mixture on to 2 warmed serving plates, lay the pepper strips on top, then arrange the chicken pieces on top of them. Pour the sauce all over.

### BRIAN TURNER

# SPINACH-STUFFED CHICKEN LEG ON TURMERIC-BRAISED POTATOES WITH CUMIN-FRIED ONIONS

Yvonne McSherry from Chester can't resist buying spices – even though she never knows what to do with them. She brought along a selection and Brian cooked up a spicy chicken dinner.

**SERVES 2**

2 large chicken legs
3 tablespoons sunflower oil
150 ml (5 fl oz) chicken stock
2 potatoes, diced
150 ml (5 fl oz) dry white wine
5 cardamom pods
50 g (2 oz) butter
1–2 teaspoons turmeric, to taste
1 tablespoon chopped fresh coriander

1 large onion, finely chopped
1 teaspoon ground cumin
Salt and freshly ground black pepper

**FOR THE STUFFING**

100 g (4 oz) fresh spinach
1 egg yolk
3 tablespoons double cream
$\frac{1}{2}$ teaspoon grated fresh root ginger
40 g ($1\frac{1}{2}$ oz) ground almonds

Pre-heat the oven to gas mark 6, 200°C (400°F).

First make the stuffing. Wash the spinach well and put it in a pan with just the water clinging to the leaves. Cook for 3–4 minutes, until wilted, then drain very thoroughly, squeezing out the excess liquid, and chop. Whisk together the egg yolk and cream, then add the spinach, ginger and ground almonds and mix well. Season with salt and pepper.

Remove the thigh bone from each chicken leg by scraping the meat down the bone and pulling it out, leaving a pocket.

Heat 2 tablespoons of the oil in a frying pan and fry the chicken legs, skin-side down, until they begin to brown. Remove from the heat and spoon the spinach stuffing into the pocket in each chicken leg, pressing it in firmly. Fold the chicken flesh up over the stuffing and secure with wooden cocktail sticks. Place each chicken leg on a square of buttered aluminium foil and pour 1 tablespoon of the stock over each one. Wrap securely in the foil, place on a baking sheet and bake in the oven for 15–20 minutes, until the chicken is cooked through.

Heat the remaining oil in a frying pan, add the diced potatoes and fry for 2 minutes. Add the wine and the remaining stock, bring to the boil, then add the cardamom pods and simmer for 5–10 minutes, or until the liquid has reduced by half and the potatoes are tender. Dice half the butter and whisk it into the potatoes with the turmeric. Stir in the coriander, then taste and adjust the seasoning if necessary.

Heat the remaining butter in a separate pan, add the onion and fry until softened but not coloured. Add the cumin and continue to cook until the onion begins to turn brown. Drain off any liquid.

To serve, arrange the onion on 2 warmed serving plates and place the chicken legs on top, removing the cocktail sticks. Surround with the potatoes and their sauce.

---

### READY STEADY COOK Tip
*After boning the chicken legs, flatten them slightly with a cleaver, mallet or rolling pin to make the pocket larger.*

---

## BRIAN TURNER

# ATLANTA CHICKEN WITH KUMQUAT CHUTNEY AND ASPARAGUS

*See photograph*

It was love at first sight for American-born Kristen Morrison when policeman Paul came to her rescue. Brian helped her concoct this Valentine's Day dish for him, while he was putting together a sumptuous dessert with Antony (see page 89).

| | |
|---|---|
| **SERVES 2** | 2 tablespoons double cream |
| 1 poussin | 1 tablespoon chopped fresh basil |
| 1 tablespoon olive oil | Salt and freshly ground black pepper |
| 25 g (1 oz) butter | |
| 4 teaspoons Dijon mustard | **FOR THE CHUTNEY** |
| 40 g (1½ oz) cashew nuts, finely ground | 2 shallots, chopped |
| 100 g (4 oz) mixed long grain and wild rice | 1 tablespoon white wine vinegar |
| 10 asparagus spears | 1 tablespoon soft brown sugar |
| 175 ml (6 fl oz) dry white wine | 8 kumquats, quartered |
| 150 ml (5 fl oz) chicken stock | |

Pre-heat the oven to gas mark 6, 200°C (400°F).

To make the chutney, place all the ingredients in a pan, partially cover with a lid and cook over a medium heat for 25–30 minutes.

To prepare the poussin, cut along each side of the backbone with a sharp knife and then remove it. Open the bird out and cut the wishbone in half, or take it out. Put the bird skin-side up on a work surface and press down sharply on the breast with the palm of your hand to flatten it. Cut the poussin in half.

Heat the oil and half the butter in a large frying pan and brown the poussin for 3 minutes on each side. Place in an ovenproof dish, skin-side up, and roast for 20–30 minutes. Half-way through the cooking time, brush the poussin with the mustard and sprinkle the ground cashew nuts on top. Check that the poussin is cooked by inserting a skewer in a leg, near the bone; if the juices run clear it is done.

Cook the rice in boiling salted water until just tender – about 20 minutes or according to the instructions on the packet. Drain and sauté in the remaining butter for 2–3 minutes.

Cut the bottom third off each asparagus spear, slice finely and set aside. Place the asparagus tips in a lightly greased ovenproof dish, pour 2 tablespoons of the white wine over them, cover and bake in the oven for 8–10 minutes. Drain the asparagus if necessary, reserving any liquid.

For the sauce, heat the chicken stock in a pan, add the remaining wine, then boil until reduced to half its original volume. Add the chopped asparagus stalks and any reserved asparagus cooking liquid and continue to cook until the asparagus is tender. Stir in the cream and heat through, then stir in the basil. Season to taste with salt and pepper.

To serve, spoon the rice into the centre of 2 warmed serving plates and put the poussin on top. Spoon the kumquat chutney around the rice and arrange the asparagus tips on top of the chutney. Surround with the sauce.

---

### READY STEADY COOK Tips

• *If the chutney becomes too dry while it is cooking, add a little water or white wine to the pan.*

• *Wild rice is not actually a rice at all but an aquatic grass, grown in North America. Its long black grains are delicious but expensive, and a good way to stretch it is to serve it with long grain white rice. Packets of mixed wild and white rice are now readily available – cook according to packet instructions.*

---

## ANTONY WORRALL THOMPSON

# BERTIE'S BUDGET VIRGIN CHICKEN WITH A LITTLE SUMMER SOUP

Chicken breasts and tomatoes stuffed with ricotta and pesto, served with sauce vierge – and perhaps a cucumber and yogurt soup to start

Marilyn Mayes from Hertfordshire asked Antony to cook chicken, her favourite ingredient, and pesto, which she'd never tried before. Antony named this summery dish after Marilyn's pet cockatiel, Bert, who's renowned for mimicking TV theme tunes and has almost mastered the *Ready Steady Cook* theme!

**SERVES 2**
4 small, firm, flavoursome tomatoes
2 boneless skinless chicken breasts
2 tablespoons olive oil
Salt and freshly ground black pepper

1 teaspoon chopped fresh sage
1 tablespoon chopped fresh
mixed parsley and basil
2 teaspoons pesto
$1/2$ small onion, finely chopped

**FOR THE SOUP (OPTIONAL)**
1 cucumber
1 tablespoon chopped onion
or spring onions
200 ml (7 fl oz) Greek yoghurt
1 tablespoon finely chopped fresh mint

**FOR THE SAUCE VIERGE**
$2^1/2$ tablespoons olive oil
1 tablespoon pesto
juice of $1/2$ lemon
3 small, flavoursome tomatoes,
de-seeded and diced
1 tablespoon chopped fresh basil
1 tablespoon chopped fresh parsley

**FOR THE STUFFING**
100 g (4 oz) ricotta cheese
1 egg yolk

If you are making the soup, extract the juice from the cucumber and onion using a centrifugal juice extractor. Whisk in the Greek yoghurt, season to taste with salt and pepper and stir in the chopped mint. Chill thoroughly before serving.

For the chicken, mix together all the ingredients for the stuffing. Pre-heat the oven to gas mark 6, 200°C (400°F).

Cut the tomatoes in half, scoop out the seeds and leave the tomato halves upside-down on a piece of kitchen paper for a few minutes to drain. Using a sharp knife, slit each chicken breast lengthwise down the centre, being careful not to cut all the way through. Use the knife to fold back the flesh and form a pocket. Stuff the chicken and the tomato halves with the ricotta mixture. Heat the oil in a frying pan, add the chicken and fry for about 5 minutes per side, until cooked through. Put the tomato halves in the oven for 5 minutes to heat through, then place under a hot grill until slightly browned.

To make the sauce, gently heat the oil in a pan, stir in the pesto and heat through, then add the lemon juice and simmer for 1–2 minutes. Add the tomatoes, basil and parsley and cook gently for 2–3 minutes longer.

To serve, arrange the chicken and tomatoes on 2 warmed serving plates and pour over the sauce.

---

### READY STEADY COOK Tips
• *If you don't have a juice extractor for the soup you could process the cucumber and onion in a blender or liquidizer, then press it through a sieve.*
• *If you have time, chill the ricotta mixture for 1–2 hours to firm up before stuffing the chicken and tomatoes.*
• *Sauce vierge is also good with grilled fish.*

---

BRIAN TURNER

# DANISH-STYLE PHEASANT WITH YORKSHIRE BUBBLE AND SQUEAK

Louisa Greenbaum lives in East London but her favourite foods are influenced by her Danish mother and by Yorkshire, where she grew up. Brian devised a fantastic pheasant dish in honour of both.

**SERVES 2**

2 pheasant breasts
1 tablespoon double cream
2 teaspoons dry white wine
1 teaspoon mustard
Salt and freshly ground black pepper
Sprigs of parsley and dill, to garnish

**FOR THE STUFFING**

2 tablespoons sunflower oil
100 g (4 oz) vacuum-packed chestnuts, roughly chopped
$^1/_2$ x 275 g (10 oz) tin of blackcurrants
1 tablespoon redcurrant jelly

**FOR THE BUBBLE AND SQUEAK**

350 g (12 oz) potatoes, diced
75 g (3 oz) Brussels sprouts, cut in half
2 tablespoons sunflower oil

**FOR THE BRANDY SAUCE**

1 tablespoon sunflower oil
1 small onion, finely chopped
300 ml (10 fl oz) chicken stock
2 tablespoons brandy
150 ml (5 fl oz) double cream
1 tablespoon finely chopped fresh parsley
1 tablespoon finely chopped fresh dill

Pre-heat the oven to gas mark 6, 200°C (400°F).

First make the stuffing. Heat the oil in a pan, add the chestnuts, drained blackcurrants and redcurrant jelly and simmer for 2–3 minutes, until the mixture is pasty in consistency. Leave to cool.

Put the pheasant breasts in a well-buttered ovenproof dish and season well. Mix together the cream, wine and mustard and spread over the pheasant breasts. Roast in the oven for 8 minutes, basting occasionally. Remove from the oven, cut a pocket in each pheasant breast and fill with the stuffing (any extra can be piled on top). Return to the oven for a further 5 minutes, until cooked through.

To make the bubble and squeak, cook the potatoes in boiling salted water until tender, adding the Brussels sprouts half-way through. Drain and mash together, then season well. Heat the oil in a frying pan and fry the potato mixture until nicely browned, tossing half-way through.

To make the sauce, heat the oil in a frying pan, add the onion and cook gently until softened. Add the stock, brandy, cream, parsley and dill and cook until reduced to about a third of its original volume. Season to taste.

To serve, place the pheasant breasts on a bed of bubble and squeak, pour the sauce over and garnish with parsley and dill sprigs.

## ANTONY WORRALL THOMPSON

# MITCH'S BI-FOCAL CHICKEN

Chicken cooked two ways with carrot rösti, sautéed vegetables and tarragon cream sauce

Rawle Beckles from London brought along a selection of his favourite ingredients. Antony cooked up a delicious chicken dish in honour of Rawle's wife Mitch.

**SERVES 2**

300 ml (10 fl oz) chicken stock
85 ml (3 fl oz) dry white wine
2 carrots, sliced
6 shallots, peeled
1 bay leaf
A small handful of fresh tarragon
2 boneless chicken breasts
1 tablespoon olive oil
25 g (1 oz) butter

100 g (4 oz) baby sweetcorn
250 ml (8 fl oz) double cream
A squeeze of lemon juice
Salt and freshly ground black pepper
Flatleaf parsley, to garnish (optional)

**FOR THE CARROT RÖSTI**

3 carrots, grated
1 tablespoon plain flour
1 tablespoon olive oil

Put the stock and white wine in a small pan and add the sliced carrots, whole shallots, bay leaf and the stalks from the tarragon. Bring to a gentle simmer, then add one chicken breast and poach for about 15 minutes, until cooked through. Leave covered in the pan.

Season the remaining chicken breast with salt and pepper. Heat the olive oil and half the butter in a small frying pan, add the chicken skin-side down and brown over a medium heat. Reduce the heat slightly and cook for about 10–15 minutes, turning half-way through.

Cook the baby sweetcorn in boiling water for 2–3 minutes, then drain, refresh in cold water and cut in half lengthways.

To make the carrot rösti, put the grated carrots and flour in a bowl, season well and mix thoroughly. Shape into 2 rounds. Heat the olive oil in a large heavy-based frying pan and carefully transfer the rösti to it, using a fish slice. Fry over a medium-high heat for about 4 minutes on each side, until brown and crisp. (If the rösti start to fall apart when you try to turn them over, cook for a little longer until really crisp underneath.) Drain on kitchen paper.

To make the sauce, pour the cream into a pan and simmer until reduced to about half its original volume. Add 4 tablespoons of the stock in which the chicken was poached and simmer for a further 3–4 minutes, stirring occasionally. Roughly chop the tarragon leaves and stir them into the sauce. Add the lemon juice and season to taste.

Heat the remaining butter in a frying pan and add the baby sweetcorn and the shallots and carrot slices from poaching the chicken. Fry over a medium heat for about 2 minutes, until golden.

To serve, slice both chicken breasts (removing the skin from the poached chicken if preferred). Place the carrot rösti on 2 warmed serving plates and arrange the sliced chicken on top. Surround with the vegetables and pour the tarragon sauce over the poached chicken and around the vegetables. Garnish with flatleaf parsley, if liked.

---

**READY STEADY COOK Tip**
*Shallots are much easier to peel if you pour boiling water over them and leave for about 30 seconds.*

---

## B R I A N   T U R N E R

# POULET FARCI LOUISE BLANDFORD

Chicken on a potato galette with green beans and
lemon butter herb sauce
*See photograph*

Louise Hawkins from Dorset loves cooking and entertaining. She hoped Brian
would help her create a wonderful dish that would persuade Steve,
her partner of 14 years, to marry her.

**SERVES 2**
15 g (¹/₂ oz) butter
2 streaky bacon rashers, finely chopped
6 button mushrooms, very finely chopped
2 boneless skinless chicken breasts
1 tablespoon plain flour, seasoned with salt
and pepper
1 egg, beaten
2 tablespoons olive oil
100 g (4 oz) green beans
Salt and freshly ground black pepper

**FOR THE POTATO GALETTES**
2 large potatoes, grated
¹/₂ onion, grated
1 tablespoon olive oil

**FOR THE SAUCE**
3 tablespoons dry white wine
Juice of ¹/₂ lemon
150 ml (5 fl oz) double cream
50 g (2 oz) chilled butter, diced
2 tablespoons chopped mixed fresh herbs such
as parsley, basil and tarragon

Melt half the butter in a pan and fry the bacon and mushrooms for
3–4 minutes, until golden. Season with salt and pepper and leave to
cool. With a sharp knife, cut a lengthwise slit down the side of each
chicken breast to form a pocket, being careful not to cut right through.
Stuff with the bacon and mushroom mixture. Coat the chicken with the
seasoned flour then dip in the beaten egg. Fry in the olive oil for
about 5 minutes on each side, until well browned and cooked through.

Meanwhile, make the potato galettes. Put the grated potatoes and onion in a bowl with some salt and pepper and mix well. Heat the olive oil in a large heavy-based frying pan and spoon in the potato and onion mixture in 2 portions, flattening them with the back of the spoon. Fry for about 5 minutes on each side, until golden brown.

Cook the green beans in boiling salted water for 3–4 minutes until just tender. Drain and set aside.

To make the sauce, put the wine and lemon juice in a pan and cook until reduced to about half the original volume. Stir in the cream and heat through. Add the butter a few pieces at a time, whisking constantly, until you have a smooth sauce. Stir in the herbs and season to taste.

To serve, melt the remaining butter in a frying pan, add the green beans and toss for 1–2 minutes just to heat through. Place the potato galettes on 2 warmed serving plates and put the chicken on top. Arrange the green beans to one side and pour the sauce all round.

---

**READY STEADY COOK Tip**
*You could include flavourings in the potato galettes, such as chopped fresh herbs, a pinch of chilli powder, caraway or cumin seeds.*

---

## ANTONY WORRALL THOMPSON

# J.J.'S MAURITIAN FANCY

Deep-fried chicken, okra, banana and sweet potatoes with chicken and pineapple fricassée

Joan Jones, nicknamed J.J., lived in Mauritius for two years, where she had been fascinated by the unusual vegetables in the local market but never dared try them. Now she's returned to Preston, she challenged Antony to recapture the Mauritian sunshine.

**SERVES 2–3**

100 g (4 oz) sweet potato, cut into 1 cm ($^1/_2$ inch) dice

Sunflower oil for deep-frying

1 boneless skinless chicken breast, cut into strips

50 g (2 oz) okra, cut lengthwise in half

1 firm banana, cut into 4 cm ($1^1/_2$ inch) chunks

2 tablespoons plain flour

**FOR THE FRICASSÉE**

100 g (4 oz) sweet potato, cut into 1 cm ($^1/_2$ inch) dice

2 tablespoons sunflower oil

1 onion, chopped

$^1/_2$ teaspoon garam masala

$^1/_2$ teaspoon chilli powder

$^1/_2$ teaspoon ground cumin

$^1/_2$ red pepper, diced

$^1/_2$ green pepper, diced

$^1/_2$ yellow pepper, diced

1 boneless skinless chicken breast, cut into strips

175 g (6 oz) fresh pineapple, diced

50 g (2 oz) okra, cut into 1 cm ($^1/_2$ inch) rounds

2–3 tablespoons crème fraîche

**FOR THE BATTER**

75 g (3 oz) plain flour

A pinch of salt

1 egg

3–4 tablespoons milk

**TO GARNISH**

A few lettuce leaves

A few lemon slices

2 tomatoes, cut into wedges

Cook all the sweet potato, including the potato for the fricassée, in boiling water for 2–3 minutes, then drain and set aside.

For the fricassée, heat the oil in a pan, add the onion and cook gently for 2 minutes. Add the spices and peppers and cook for 2 minutes, then add the chicken, pineapple, okra and 100 g (4 oz) of the par-boiled sweet potato. Simmer gently for 10–15 minutes, until everything is tender, then stir in the crème fraîche and heat through gently.

For the batter, put the flour and salt in a bowl and whisk in the egg, then gradually whisk in enough milk to give the consistency of double cream.

Heat the oil for deep-frying in a saucepan or deep-fat fryer. Coat the chicken pieces, okra, banana and par-boiled sweet potato in the flour and shake off any excess. Dip the chicken in the batter and deep-fry for about 7 minutes, until golden brown and cooked through. Drain on kitchen paper and keep warm. Dip the okra, banana and sweet potato in the remaining batter and deep-fry for about 3 minutes, until golden brown. Drain on kitchen paper.

To serve, arrange the lettuce leaves, lemon slices and tomato wedges around the edge of a serving platter and pile the fried chicken and vegetables in the centre. Serve with the chicken and pineapple fricassée, accompanied by rice or bread.

---

### READY STEADY COOK Tips
- *To check whether the oil is hot enough for deep frying, put in a small cube of bread. If it turns golden brown in about 20 seconds the oil is the correct temperature.*
- *The chicken and pineapple fricassée makes a meal in itself if you serve it with some rice.*

---

## BRIAN TURNER

# HONEY AND LIME CHICKEN WITH ROASTED CELERIAC, CHICKEN LIVER MOUSSE AND MUSHROOM SAUCE

Maureen Travis from Colchester is mother to a very special bouquet – daughters Daisy, Lily, Fleur and Poppy. Brian showed her an ingenious way of serving chicken and chicken livers to make a delicious dish for the whole family.

**SERVES 2**
2 boneless skinless chicken breasts
3 tablespoons runny honey
Juice of $^1/_2$ lime
Rind of 2 limes
350 g (12 oz) celeriac
2 tablespoons sunflower oil
3 bacon rashers, cut into thin strips
Salt and freshly ground black pepper

**FOR THE MOUSSE**
100 g (4 oz) chicken livers
$1^1/_2$ tablespoons double cream
1 size-1 egg

**FOR THE MUSHROOM SAUCE**
300 ml (10 fl oz) vegetable stock
1 tablespoon dry white wine
4 tablespoons double cream
5 mushrooms, very thinly sliced
25 g (1 oz) butter
1 tablespoon chopped fresh dill

Pre-heat the oven to gas mark 6, 200°C (400°F).
First make the chicken liver mousse. Blend the chicken livers in a food processor until smooth. Add the cream and egg and continue to blend until thoroughly combined. Season with salt and pepper and pour into 2 lightly greased small dariole moulds or ramekin dishes.

Place in a roasting tin, pour enough boiling water into the tin to come two-thirds of the way up the sides of the moulds and bake for about 25 minutes, until the mousse is set.

Coat the chicken with the honey and place in a shallow heatproof dish. Pour over the lime juice and sprinkle with the rind. Leave to marinate for about 10 minutes, if you have time, then cook under a hot grill for 15 minutes, basting regularly and turning half-way through.

Peel the celeriac and scoop it into balls using a melon baller, or cut it into small cubes. Toss it in half the oil, season and then place in a baking tin and roast in the oven for 15–20 minutes. Heat the remaining oil in a pan and fry the bacon until crisp. Add the roasted celeriac and cook for a further 5 minutes, until well browned.

For the mushroom sauce, pour the vegetable stock into a pan and boil over a high heat until reduced to half its original volume. Stir in the white wine, cream, mushrooms, butter and dill and cook gently for 1–2 minutes. Season to taste.

To serve, put the chicken on 2 warmed serving plates and arrange the celeriac and bacon next to it. Run a knife around the edge of each mousse to loosen it, turn it out and place on top of the celeriac mixture, then spoon the mushroom sauce over the mousse.

---

### READY STEADY COOK Tips
• Most chicken livers come ready trimmed these days but, if necessary, cut off any tubes or membranes and green patches before use. Any leftover livers will freeze well.
• If your food processor is too large to purée such small quantities for the chicken liver mousse, use a liquidizer or a hand blender.
• If you have time to prepare it in advance, leave the chicken to marinate for several hours, covered, in the refrigerator.

---

## BRIAN TURNER

# STUFFED TURKEY STEAKS WITH BEAN STEW AND DINO PASTA

Janet Brook now lives in Cornwall but originally came from Yorkshire, and was keen to cook with a fellow Yorkshireman. As the ultimate challenge, Janet's grandson had insisted she bring along dinosaur-shaped pasta, saying, 'Brian will know what to do with it.'

**SERVES 2**

2 x 175 g (6 oz) thick turkey breast steaks
1 tablespoon olive oil
25 g (1 oz) butter
Juice of $1/2$ lemon
Salt and freshly ground black pepper

**FOR THE PASTA**

50 g (2 oz) dinosaur pasta or other pasta shapes
1 tablespoon olive oil
3 plum tomatoes, quartered
15 g ($1/2$ oz) butter

**FOR THE BEAN STEW**

4 tablespoons olive oil
1 small aubergine, finely diced
1 garlic clove, crushed
3 slices of ham, finely diced
1 x 425 g (15 oz) tin of haricot beans, drained
2 tablespoons double cream
2 tablespoons chopped fresh basil

**FOR THE FRIED ONIONS**

Sunflower oil for deep-frying
1 onion, sliced
2 tablespoons milk
25–50 g (1–2 oz) plain flour, seasoned with salt and pepper

Cook the pasta in boiling salted water for about 8 minutes or until *al dente*, then drain and set aside.

Carefully cut a lengthwise slit in each turkey steak to form a pocket (like pitta bread). Drizzle the olive oil over them and cook on a ridged grill pan or in a heavy-based frying pan for 6–10 minutes on each side, depending on their thickness.

To make the bean stew, heat the oil in a pan, add the aubergine and fry for 3 minutes. Add the garlic and ham, season with salt and pepper and cook for 5 minutes longer. Stir in the haricot beans and heat through. Add the cream and simmer for 2–3 minutes, then add the basil. Taste and adjust the seasoning if necessary. Spoon 2 tablespoons of the bean stew into the pocket of each turkey steak and keep warm in a low oven.

For the pasta, heat the olive oil in a frying pan, add the tomatoes and fry for 3 minutes. Stir in the drained pasta and the butter, season to taste and toss well.

For the fried onions, heat the sunflower oil in a saucepan or deep-fat fryer. Dip the onion slices in the milk and then in the seasoned flour and deep-fry until golden brown. Drain on kitchen paper.

Melt the butter in a small pan, then remove from the heat and stir in the lemon juice.

To serve, spoon the bean stew on to 2 warmed serving plates. Pile the pasta mixture on top and arrange the stuffed turkey steaks on top of that. Pour over the lemon butter and garnish with the fried onions.

---

**READY STEADY COOK Tip**
*Pork steaks could be substituted for the turkey steaks.
If they are very thin, there is no need to stuff them.*

---

# MEAT DISHES

MATA HARI'S MOTHER'S MEZE – 54

HAM WITH HOT PINEAPPLE CHUTNEY – 55

AINSLEY'S ALTERNATIVE MUNCH BRUNCH
WITH A CRUNCH – 57

BOEUF GRILLÉ, SALADE DE CHAMPIGNONS,
SAUCE HOLLANDAISE – 59

TOYS AREN'T US – 61

TINA TURNER'S BREAKFAST – 62

JET-LAG STEAK STACK – 63

THE HUMBER BRIDGE VEGETABLE HOTPOT – 65

LYNN'S STEAK OF MANY COLOURS – 67

PORK SPÄTZLE – 69

SPAGHETTI BOLOGNESE BLACK WATCH BEETLE – 70

FILLET OF PORK TOUT LE MONDE – 71

FARFALLE CARBONARA – 72

BLACK PUDDING À LA FORESTIÈRE WITH
PIEDMONTESE PEPPERS – 73

POTIRON À LA FLAMANDE – 74

AGNEAU AU FER À LA COMPOTE DES FRUITS – 76

ALISON'S HOT AND SPICY DREAM – 77

## A N T O N Y   W O R R A L L   T H O M P S O N

# MATA HARI'S MOTHER'S MEZE

Chick pea salad, couscous salad with spicy sausage, and grilled vegetables with yoghurt dip

Pauline Robinson lives in Marlow, Buckinghamshire, but her husband works in Turkey. She brought along a selection of Mediterranean and Middle Eastern ingredients and Antony cooked up three tasty dishes.

**SERVES 2**
1 courgette, sliced lengthwise
1 small head of radicchio, cut into wedges
1 tablespoon olive oil
A few lettuce leaves
175 g (6 oz) kabanos sausage
(spicy cured sausage), sliced
1 tablespoon chopped fresh parsley
1 tablespoon balsamic vinegar
Salt and freshly ground black pepper

**FOR THE COUSCOUS SALAD**
100 g (4 oz) couscous
1 courgette, sliced
A pinch of ground coriander
A pinch of ground turmeric
A pinch of ground cinnamon
40 g (1½ oz) sultanas
3 small tomatoes, finely diced
1 tablespoon olive oil

**FOR THE CHICK PEA SALAD**
1 x 425 g (15 oz) tin of chick peas, drained
A pinch of ground coriander
A pinch of ground turmeric
2 pinches of ground cumin
A pinch of ground cinnamon
2 tablespoons olive oil
¼ small onion, finely chopped
3 small tomatoes, cut into quarters
and de-seeded
1 tablespoon chopped fresh basil
1 tablespoon balsamic vinegar
2 tablespoons chopped fresh coriander

**FOR THE YOGHURT DIP**
¼ cucumber, peeled, de-seeded
and finely diced
2 teaspoons chopped fresh mint
150 ml (5 fl oz) Greek yoghurt

For the couscous salad, put the couscous in a bowl, pour over hot water to cover and leave for about 10 minutes, until the couscous is tender and the water has been absorbed. Lightly boil or steam the courgette until just tender. Mix together the couscous, spices, courgette, sultanas, tomatoes and olive oil, then season to taste.

For the chick pea salad, mix together all the ingredients except 1 tablespoon of the fresh coriander and season with salt and pepper.

For the yoghurt dip, mix together all the ingredients and season with salt and pepper.

Brush the courgette slices and radicchio wedges with the olive oil and cook under a hot grill for about 1 minute per side, until the courgette is golden brown and the radicchio is slightly softened.

To serve, put the lettuce leaves on a plate and spoon the couscous salad on top. Arrange the sausage slices on top of the salad and sprinkle with the parsley. Put the chick pea salad in a bowl and garnish with the remaining coriander. Arrange the grilled radicchio and courgette on a plate and drizzle over the balsamic vinegar. Serve with the yoghurt dip.

B R I A N   T U R N E R

# HAM WITH HOT PINEAPPLE CHUTNEY

Katrina Mudge from Newbury wanted Brian to show her how to cook sweet with savoury, so she brought along some gammon, pineapple and sweet potatoes.

| SERVES 2 | 75 g (3 oz) butter |
|---|---|
| 100 g (4 oz) spring greens, finely shredded, plus 4–6 whole leaves | 1 small onion, sliced |
| 3 tablespoons white wine vinegar | 2 tablespoons honey |
| 1/2 pineapple (about 225 g/8 oz) | 300 g (11 oz) gammon steak, cut into 4 medallions |
| 300 g (11 oz) sweet potatoes | Salt and freshly ground black pepper |

Pre-heat the oven to gas mark 4, 180°C (350°F).

Put the shredded spring greens in a serving dish. Bring the vinegar to the boil in a small pan and pour it over the greens. Leave to soak for about 15 minutes.

Peel the pineapple. Finely dice half the flesh and cut the rest into 2.5 cm (1 inch) rounds with a pastry cutter or cut into wedges. Peel the sweet potatoes and cut them into slices 1 cm ($^1/_2$ inch thick). Cut these into 2.5 cm (1 inch) rounds or into wedges, like the pineapple. Cook the sweet potatoes in boiling salted water for 5 minutes until just tender, then drain and set aside.

To make the pineapple chutney, melt 25 g (1 oz) of the butter in a small pan, add the finely diced pineapple and cook for 3 minutes. Add the onion and honey and cook gently for about 10 minutes, until the onion is soft. Season to taste with salt and pepper.

Cut the stalks out of the whole spring green leaves, then blanch the leaves in a frying pan of boiling water for 1–2 minutes, until just softened. Drain, then spread flat and pat dry. Place 1 tablespoon of the chutney in the centre of each leaf, then wrap up to form a parcel. Place in a shallow ovenproof dish with 25 g (1 oz) of the butter and bake for about 5 minutes, until the butter has melted.

Heat the remaining butter in a frying pan, add the sweet potatoes and the pineapple circles or wedges and cook until golden brown on both sides.

Cook the gammon on a lightly oiled ridged grill pan or in a heavy frying pan for 4–5 minutes on each side.

To serve, arrange alternate pieces of pineapple and sweet potato in an overlapping circle around the edge of each serving plate. Place the gammon and the chutney parcels in the middle and pour the melted butter from the parcels over the top. The shredded spring greens should be served separately as a salad.

---

### READY STEADY COOK Tip

*Make some extra pineapple chutney and serve it with other meat dishes. It will keep in the fridge for up to a week.*

---

## ANTONY WORRALL THOMPSON

# AINSLIE'S ALTERNATIVE MUNCH BRUNCH WITH A CRUNCH

Baked brioche filled with pork and sage patties, mushrooms, bacon-wrapped tomatoes, fried eggs and fried onion rings

Sue Hansen's husband likes nothing more than a fry-up of his favourite ingredients – sausage, bacon, eggs and mushrooms. Antony created a bumper breakfast dish that's delicious at any time of day.

**SERVES 4**

1 brioche loaf or 8 individual brioches
6 streaky bacon rashers, rinds removed
6 small tomatoes, cut in half
15 g ( $^1/_2$ oz) butter
100 g (4 oz) button mushrooms
$^1/_2$ teaspoon chopped fresh sage
A squeeze of lemon juice
4 eggs
1 tablespoon sunflower oil
Salt and freshly ground black pepper

**FOR THE FRIED ONION RINGS**

100 g (4 oz) plain flour, plus extra for dusting
1 egg
150 ml (5 fl oz) milk
Sunflower oil for deep-frying
1 onion, sliced into rings

**FOR THE PATTIES**

450 g (1 lb) sausagemeat
2 teaspoons chopped fresh sage
$^1/_2$ teaspoon ground coriander
1 tablespoon olive oil

Pre-heat the oven to gas mark 6, 200°C (400°F).

If you are using a brioche loaf, slice it in half lengthwise and, leaving the crust intact, scoop out the centre. If you are using individual brioches, cut off the tops and scoop out the centre. Process the scooped-out brioche in a food processor or liquidizer to make breadcrumbs. Place the 2 brioche halves or the individual brioches in the oven for about 5 minutes, until just beginning to brown.

Next make the batter for the fried onion rings. Whisk together the flour, egg and milk, season with salt and pepper and set aside.

For the patties, mix together the sausagemeat, sage and coriander, season and knead lightly. Shape into 8 small patties and coat with the brioche crumbs (you may not need them all). Fry in the olive oil for about 5 minutes on each side, until browned and cooked through.

Stretch the bacon rashers by running the back of a knife along each one, then cut them in half. Wrap 1 piece of bacon around each tomato half, put on long skewers and place under a hot grill until the bacon is cooked and the tomato halves soft.

Heat the butter in a small pan, add the mushrooms, sage and lemon juice and fry for 3–4 minutes until softened, then season.

For the onion rings, heat the oil for deep-frying in a saucepan or deep-fat fryer. Dust the onion rings with flour, dip them in the batter and deep-fry for 1–2 minutes, until golden brown. Drain well on kitchen paper.

Heat the tablespoon of sunflower oil in a pan and fry the eggs.

To serve, fill the brioche halves with the bacon-wrapped tomatoes, mushrooms and meat patties and put the fried eggs on top (if using small brioches put the tomatoes and mushrooms inside and place the meat patties and fried eggs beside them). Garnish with the onion rings.

---

### *READY STEADY COOK Tip*
*If you don't have time to make the batter for the onion rings, just dip them in a little milk, then a little seasoned flour, before deep-frying.*

---

## BRIAN TURNER

# BOEUF GRILLÉ, SALADE DE CHAMPIGNONS, SAUCE HOLLANDAISE

### Spicy beef steak with warm mushroom salad and hollandaise sauce

Rachel O'Hara, a colour consultant from Billericay, Essex, brought along some stylish ingredients and Brian cooked a meal that looked as good as it tasted.

**SERVES 2**

1 teaspoon ground coriander
1 teaspoon ground cumin
1 teaspoon paprika
1 teaspoon cayenne pepper
2 x 175 g (6 oz) sirloin steaks
4 tablespoons olive oil
6 shallots, peeled
1 tablespoon caster sugar
1 large or 2 medium potatoes, thinly sliced lengthwise
100 g (4 oz) green beans, cut into 1 cm ($1/2$ inch) lengths
Salt and freshly ground black pepper

**FOR THE MUSHROOM SALAD**

1 tablespoon olive oil
150 g (5 oz) oyster mushrooms, sliced
1 tablespoon white wine vinegar

**FOR THE HOLLANDAISE SAUCE**

1 size-1 egg yolk
2 teaspoons white wine vinegar
100 g (4 oz) butter, melted
1 tablespoon chopped fresh parsley

Pre-heat the oven to gas mark 6, 200°C (400°F).

Mix together the spices and coat the steaks with them. Heat 1 tablespoon of the oil in a heavy-based frying pan and fry the steaks for 3–5 minutes on each side, depending on how you like them done.

Cook the shallots in a pan of boiling water for 3–5 minutes, until softened. Drain and pat dry, then place in a small casserole dish or ovenproof frying pan with 1 tablespoon of the olive oil, sprinkle with the sugar and fry for about 2 minutes. Transfer to the oven and cook for 10 minutes, until golden.

Heat the remaining oil in a frying pan and fry the potato slices until tender and golden brown, adding salt and pepper to taste.

Meanwhile, make the mushroom salad. Heat the oil in a frying pan, add the mushrooms and fry for 2–3 minutes, until tender. Transfer the mushrooms to a small bowl, season with salt and pepper and then stir in the vinegar and 1 tablespoon of water.

Cook the green beans in boiling salted water for 3–4 minutes, until just tender, then drain and season. Keep warm.

To make the hollandaise sauce, whisk the egg yolk, vinegar and $^1/_2$ tablespoon of water together in a small pan for 3 minutes over a very gentle heat. Slowly add the melted butter, whisking continuously, until the sauce thickens but still has a pouring consistency. Season to taste and stir in the parsley.

To serve, arrange the fried potatoes and shallots on 2 warmed serving plates. Pile the beans in the centre and put the steaks on top. Spoon the mushroom salad around the outside and pour the hollandaise sauce over the steaks.

---

### READY STEADY COOK Tip

*Hollandaise sauce is not as difficult to make as many people think and is very quick. The secret is to add the melted butter in a very thin stream and to keep the heat as low as possible, otherwise the egg will scramble. Keep lifting the pan off the heat as you add the butter, to prevent the mixture getting too hot.*

## ANTONY WORRALL THOMPSON

# TOYS AREN'T US

### Pork and new potato pie with red Leicester cheese

**Zoë Stewart from Norfolk has two children who refuse to eat anything she cooks for them. Antony devised an imaginative dish they wouldn't be able to resist.**

| | |
|---|---|
| **SERVES 3–4** | 150 ml (5 fl oz) dry white wine or stock |
| 675 g (1¹/₂ lb) new potatoes | 25 g (1 oz) butter |
| 2 tablespoons olive oil | 450 g (1 lb) minced pork |
| 2 shallots, finely chopped | 1 tablespoon tomato purée |
| 3 garlic cloves, finely chopped | 100 g (4 oz) red Leicester cheese, grated |
| 1 x 400 g (14 oz) tin of chopped tomatoes | Salt and freshly ground black pepper |
| 1 teaspoon dried thyme or Italian mixed herbs | |

Cut 350 g (12 oz) of the potatoes lengthwise in half and roughly chop the rest. Cook them separately in boiling salted water until tender and then drain.

Heat half the oil in a frying pan and fry the shallots and two-thirds of the garlic for about 5 minutes, until soft. Add the tomatoes, dried herbs and white wine or stock and simmer for 10–12 minutes. Season with salt and pepper.

Heat the butter and the remaining oil in a separate pan, add the minced pork and cook until browned. Add the remaining garlic and cook for 2–3 minutes, then stir in the tomato purée and tomato sauce and continue to simmer for about 15 minutes, until the pork is completely cooked.

Put the chopped potatoes in a shallow ovenproof dish large enough to hold them in a single layer. Spread the pork mixture on top and arrange the halved potatoes, cut-side up, on top of that. Cover with the grated cheese and place in a hot oven or under a hot grill for 5 minutes, until the cheese has melted.

## BRIAN TURNER

# TINA TURNER'S BREAKFAST

Fried kidneys and bacon on carrot purée with mushroom
and coriander sauce

To the embarrassment of her grandchildren, Rita Jones from Abberley, Worcestershire, did an
impromptu impression of her favourite singer, Tina Turner. Meanwhile Brian was busy
cooking her favourite ingredients – kidneys and bacon.

**SERVES 2**
225 g (8 oz) carrots, sliced
3 tablespoons Greek yoghurt
450 g (1 lb) lamb's kidneys
25 g (1 oz) butter
2 tablespoons olive oil
1 small onion, sliced
2 bacon rashers, thinly sliced
2 tablespoons thinly sliced fresh basil

Salt and freshly ground black pepper

**FOR THE SAUCE**
300 ml (10 fl oz) chicken stock
2 tablespoons damson wine or sweet sherry
25 g (1 oz) butter
6 small open-cap mushrooms, sliced
2 tablespoons chopped fresh coriander

Cook the carrots in boiling salted water until tender, then drain. Add
the Greek yoghurt and some salt and pepper, then mash until smooth.
Keep warm.

Drain the kidneys over a bowl, slice them in half lengthways and
remove the white core and the fat. Heat the butter and half the oil in
a pan and fry the kidneys for 4–5 minutes; they should be browned
on the outside but still pink in the centre.

Meanwhile, make the sauce. Put the chicken stock and wine or
sherry in a pan and boil until reduced to half its original volume. Heat
the butter in a separate pan, add the mushrooms and fry for 3–4
minutes, until tender. Drain and add them to the reduced stock with
the coriander. Season to taste and keep warm.

Fry the onion in the remaining oil for 3–4 minutes, until softened, then add the bacon, raise the heat and cook for a further 3 minutes to brown the onion and crisp the bacon.

To serve, spread the carrot purée on 2 warmed serving plates and arrange the fried bacon and onion on top. Place the kidneys on top of the bacon mixture and pour the sauce around the edge and over the kidneys. Sprinkle the basil over the top.

ANTONY WORRALL THOMPSON

# JET-LAG STEAK STACK

*Antony had stepped off a plane from Australia only hours earlier but was still able to rustle up this stunning meal for Jane Saxon from Thornton Cleveleys, Lancashire.*

**SERVES 2**

175 g (6 oz) very thin slices of fillet steak (8–10 slices)

1 x 100 g (4 oz) Mozzarella cheese in water, drained and cut into 8 slices

6 basil leaves, shredded

Salt and freshly ground black pepper

**FOR THE TOMATO SAUCE**

3 tablespoons olive oil

1 onion, finely chopped

2 garlic cloves, finely chopped

1 teaspoon dried thyme

1 x 400 g (14 oz) tin of chopped tomatoes

**FOR THE POTATO PANCAKES**

350 g (12 oz) potatoes, grated

50 g (2 oz) butter, melted

2 tablespoons olive oil

**FOR THE GREEN BEAN SALAD**

100 g (4 oz) green beans

2 tablespoons finely chopped onion

2 tablespoons olive oil

2 teaspoons balsamic vinegar

First make the tomato sauce. Heat the olive oil in a frying pan and fry the onion for 3 minutes, then stir in the garlic and thyme. Add the tomatoes and simmer for 8–10 minutes. Season with salt and pepper.

For the potato pancakes, dry the grated potatoes on kitchen paper, then mix with the melted butter and some salt and pepper. Heat the oil in a large frying pan and spoon in the potato mixture in 2 portions, flattening them with the back of the spoon. Fry for 4–5 minutes on each side, until golden and crisp. Remove from the pan and keep warm.

For the salad, cook the green beans in boiling salted water for about 4 minutes, until just tender, then drain and refresh under cold running water. Mix with the onion, oil and balsamic vinegar. Toss together lightly and season to taste.

Season the steaks and cook them quickly on both sides in the pan in which the potato pancakes were cooked; they should take only 30 seconds to 1 minute, depending on thickness.

Assemble the steak stacks as follows: put each potato cake on a heatproof plate and arrange alternate layers of steak, Mozzarella and a little tomato sauce on top, ending with a large slice of Mozzarella. Place under the grill or in a very hot oven for a few minutes until the cheese melts.

To serve, put the green bean salad beside the steak stacks and pour the remaining tomato sauce on top. Garnish with the basil.

---

### READY STEADY COOK Tips

- If you prefer a smoother texture, purée the tomato sauce in a liquidizer or food processor.
- Balsamic vinegar has a rich, mellow, sour-sweet flavour and, although it isn't cheap, a little goes a long way. Just a few drops will perk up many dishes, such as salads, fish and meat and even fresh strawberries.

B R I A N   T U R N E R

# THE HUMBER BRIDGE VEGETABLE HOTPOT

### Meatballs with couscous, vegetables and mint and yoghurt sauce
### *See photograph*

Mother-of-four Beverley Beedham from South Humberside is used to cooking on a tight budget. Brian showed her how to turn meatballs and couscous into a North African feast that doesn't break the bank.

**SERVES 2**
300 ml (10 fl oz) beef stock
150 ml (5 fl oz) dry white wine
100 g (4 oz) couscous
50 g (2 oz) butter
1 courgette, diced
1 large tomato, diced
2 carrots, diced
100 g (4 oz) frozen broad beans
1 x 425 g (15 oz) tin of chick peas, drained
Salt and freshly ground black pepper
Flatleaf parsley, to garnish

**FOR THE SAUCE**
1 tablespoon finely chopped fresh mint
4 tablespoons double cream
juice of 1/2 lemon
4 tablespoons Greek yoghurt

**FOR THE MEATBALLS**
225 g (8 oz) minced steak
1 tablespoon grated onion
1 egg yolk
1–2 teaspoons Worcestershire sauce, to taste

First make the sauce. Put all the ingredients into a bowl, season with salt and pepper and stir well to combine. Set aside.

Pour the beef stock and wine into a shallow saucepan or a frying pan and heat to simmering point. Place the couscous in a bowl and pour over boiling water to cover. Add a little of the hot stock, then cover with cling film and leave for 10 minutes, until the couscous is softened and all the liquid has been absorbed.

For the meatballs, mix together all the ingredients with some salt and pepper. Shape into 2.5 cm (1 inch) balls and poach in the simmering stock for about 5 minutes or until just cooked through (remove one from the pan and test with a knife).

Heat 25 g (1 oz) of the butter in a frying pan, add the courgette and tomato and cook gently for about 5 minutes, until the courgette is just tender. Season to taste and keep warm. Cook the carrots and broad beans separately in boiling salted water until just tender, then drain. Melt half the remaining butter in a pan, add the broad beans and the drained chick peas and toss until the chick peas are heated through. Toss the carrots in the remaining butter.

To serve, arrange the couscous on a heated serving platter, place the meatballs on top and spoon over the yoghurt sauce. Arrange the vegetables in small piles around the edge and garnish with flatleaf parsley.

---

### READY STEADY COOK Tips

• *Couscous stews are traditionally served with harissa, a fiery North African spice paste. Add $1/2$ teaspoon, or to taste, to the meatballs or the yoghurt sauce, if liked.*

• *Other vegetables can be substituted for the courgette, carrots and broad beans, such as peppers, fennel, leeks or green beans.*

---

## ANTONY WORRALL THOMPSON

# LYNN'S STEAK OF MANY COLOURS

Steak and ratatouille with polenta and grilled vegetables
*See photograph*

Lynn Manning from Newcastle upon Tyne was keen to cook something colourful to impress her partner, Paul. Polenta, red pepper and aubergine fitted the bill perfectly – and are just the sort of ingredients Antony enjoys cooking with.

**SERVES 2**

| | |
|---|---|
| 175 g (6 oz) quick-cook polenta | 1 teaspoon dried thyme |
| 450 ml (15 fl oz) water | 1 teaspoon dried oregano |
| 2 courgettes | 4 tablespoons dry white wine |
| 1 large aubergine | 2 tablespoons tomato purée |
| 1 red pepper | 2 x 150 g (5 oz) fillet steaks |
| 2 tablespoons olive oil | 1 tablespoon chopped fresh basil |
| $^1/_2$ onion, finely chopped | 1 teaspoon chopped fresh thyme |
| 4 garlic cloves, finely chopped | Salt and freshly ground black pepper |

Cook the polenta in the water with a pinch of salt according to the instructions on the packet. Spoon it into an oiled 18 x 28 x 2.5 cm (7 x 11 x 1 inch) baking tin and spread out in a layer about 2 cm ($^3/_4$ inch) thick. Leave to cool, then use a pastry cutter to cut out 4 circles 10 cm (4 inch) in diameter.

Dice 1 courgette and cut the other on the diagonal into slices 1 cm ($^1/_2$ inch) thick. Cut 4 slices from the aubergine, 1 cm ($^1/_2$ inch) thick, and dice the rest. Set aside.

Cut the red pepper in half and remove the seeds, then trim each half into a neat square; dice the trimmings. Cook the red pepper squares under a hot grill for 10 minutes, until the skin chars and blisters. Leave until cool enough to handle, then peel off the skin.

For the ratatouille, heat the oil in a pan, add the onion, garlic, red pepper trimmings, dried thyme and oregano and cook gently until the onion is translucent. Add the diced courgette and aubergine and cook for 4 minutes. Stir in the wine and tomato purée, season with salt and pepper, then cover and simmer for 20–30 minutes, adding a little water if the mixture becomes too dry.

Cook the courgette and aubergine slices on a lightly oiled ridged grill pan for about 7 minutes, until browned (or brush them with oil and cook them under the grill). Remove from the pan and keep warm.

Season the steak. Cook the steak and the polenta circles on a ridged grill pan or under a hot grill. The steak will take about 3 minutes on each side (for rare steak); the polenta circles are done when they form a golden crust.

To serve, build 2 stacks by layering a polenta circle, aubergine slice, pepper square, aubergine slice, courgette slices, polenta circle. Place each stack on a serving plate, spoon the ratatouille to one side and arrange the steak on top of the ratatouille. Sprinkle the steak with the basil and fresh thyme.

---

### *READY STEADY COOK Tips*

• *After grilling the red pepper, put it in a plastic bag for a few minutes and seal. The steam created softens the pepper, making it easier to peel.*

• *To use up the polenta trimmings, cut them into pieces and layer in a casserole dish with a well-flavoured cheese sauce, or with a tomato sauce and sliced cheese such as gorgonzola or Parmesan. Bake in the oven at gas mark 6, 200°C (400°F) until brown and bubbling.*

• *Any leftover ratatouille will keep in the fridge for several days and can be used to fill tarts or omelettes or tossed with pasta.*

# MEAT DISHES

## BRIAN TURNER

# PORK SPÄTZLE

Pork in mushroom and soured cream sauce with noodles
and green cabbage

Forever bickering about who was the better cook, mother and daughter Jenny and Ruth
Mortimer from Wilmslow, Cheshire, challenged one another on *Ready Steady Cook*. Brian
cooked Jenny this tasty pork dish with German noodles.

**SERVES 2**

1 tablespoon olive oil
50 g (2 oz) butter
1 small onion, chopped
225–275 g (8–10 oz) pork fillet, cut into
1 cm (½ inch) cubes
100 g (4 oz) button mushrooms, quartered
2 teaspoons paprika
250 ml (8 fl oz) soured cream
Lemon juice, to taste
175 g (6 oz) spätzle (German noodles) or
other dried noodles
175 g (6 oz) green cabbage, finely shredded
1 tablespoon chopped fresh parsley
Salt and freshly ground black pepper

Heat the oil and half the butter in a frying pan, add the onion and
cook gently until soft. Add the pork and cook until it is beginning to
brown, then stir in the mushrooms and cook for 5 minutes. Cover and
cook for 5–10 minutes longer, until the pork is tender. Stir in the
paprika and cook for 1 minute, then season with salt and pepper. Stir
in the soured cream and heat through but do not allow the mixture to
boil. Add lemon juice to taste.

Cook the noodles in boiling salted water until just tender (dried
spätzle will take about 15 minutes; other noodles only 8–10 minutes).
Drain and toss with half the remaining butter and some salt and pepper.

Cook the cabbage in boiling salted water for 2 minutes, then drain.
Return it to the pan and stir in the remaining butter.

To serve, arrange small piles of the noodles and cabbage around
the edges of 2 warmed serving plates. Spoon the pork and mushroom
mixture into the centre and sprinkle over the chopped parsley.

## ANTONY WORRALL THOMPSON

# SPAGHETTI BOLOGNESE BLACK WATCH BEETLE

*See photograph*

Kathleen Fiddes' family in Midlothian, Scotland, love pasta but she'd run out of ideas on how to cook it. Antony gave her plenty of inspiration with this recipe and the one on page 72.

| | |
|---|---|
| **SERVES 4** | 1 tablespoon tomato purée |
| 2 tablespoons olive oil | 4 tablespoons red wine |
| 2 onions, chopped | 1 tablespoon chopped fresh parsley |
| 3 garlic cloves, crushed | 5 drops of Tabasco sauce |
| 2 teaspoons mixed dried herbs | 450 g (1 lb) spaghetti |
| 675 g (1½ lb) minced beef | 2 tablespoons chopped fresh basil |
| 1 beef stock cube | Salt and freshly ground black pepper |
| 1 x 400 g (14 oz) tin of chopped tomatoes | Freshly grated Parmesan cheese, to serve |

Heat the oil in a pan, add the onions and cook gently until translucent.

Add the garlic, mixed herbs and minced beef and cook for 5 minutes, until the meat is browned. Crumble in the stock cube and stir in the tomatoes, tomato purée, red wine, parsley and Tabasco. Season and simmer for at least 10 minutes, until the mince is completely cooked. Ideally, if you have time, add a little water and cook slowly for 40 minutes until the sauce has thickened and reduced. Taste and adjust the seasoning, if necessary.

Cook the spaghetti in a large pan of boiling salted water for 8 minutes or until *al dente*, then drain.

To serve, pour the sauce over the spaghetti, sprinkle with the basil and accompany with the Parmesan cheese.

## BRIAN TURNER

# FILLET OF PORK TOUT LE MONDE

Pork with mixed vegetables and mushroom and prune sauce
*See photograph*

Vicky Potter from Uxbridge was lacking in ideas when it came to cooking pork. Brian changed all that when he combined pork and prunes to make a dish her RAF family adored.

**SERVES 2**
3 celery sticks, cut in half
3 tablespoons olive oil
1 onion, cut into rings
1 green pepper, sliced
$1/2$ teaspoon chilli powder
1 small egg
$1^1/_2$ tablespoons double cream
350 g (12 oz) piece of pork fillet, cut in half and fat removed
2 tablespoons plain flour, seasoned with salt and pepper
25 g (1 oz) butter

Salt and freshly ground black pepper
Chopped fresh parsley, to garnish

**FOR THE SAUCE**
75 g (3 oz) chilled butter
100 g (4 oz) button mushrooms, chopped
8 ready-to-eat prunes, chopped
300 ml (10 fl oz) chicken stock
2 tablespoons dry white wine
2 tablespoons double cream
4 tablespoons white wine vinegar
1 teaspoon grainy or Dijon mustard

First make the sauce. Heat 25 g (1 oz) of the butter in a pan, add the mushrooms and fry for 2–3 minutes, until just tender. Add the prunes and fry for 1 minute, then remove the pan from the heat and set aside. Put the stock and white wine into a separate pan and boil until reduced to just under half its original volume. Add the cream and simmer for a few minutes until it is slightly reduced.

In a small pan, boil the vinegar until it is reduced to 1 tablespoon. Add to the sauce with the mustard. Cut up the remaining butter and whisk it into the sauce a few pieces at a time, until smooth. Simmer the sauce again until reduced to about 150 ml (5 fl oz). Stir in the mushrooms and prunes and season to taste with salt and pepper. Keep warm.

Cook the celery in boiling water for 10 minutes, then drain.

Heat 2 tablespoons of the olive oil in a frying pan and fry the onion and green pepper with the chilli powder until softened. Meanwhile, lightly whisk together the egg and cream. Flatten the pork fillet slightly with the palm of your hand, then coat it in the seasoned flour, shaking off any excess. Dip the meat in the egg and cream and then fry in the butter and the remaining oil for about 8–10 minutes, turning the fillets over half-way through.

To serve, arrange the vegetables on 2 warmed serving plates, place the pork on top and pour over the sauce. Garnish with parsley.

ANTONY WORRALL THOMPSON

# **FARFALLE CARBONARA**

*See photograph*

| SERVES 4 | 2 egg yolks |
|---|---|
| 450 g (1 lb) dried farfalle pasta | 300 ml (10 fl oz) double cream |
| 1 tablespoon olive oil | 1 tablespoon chopped fresh parsley |
| 6 bacon rashers, finely sliced | 2 tablespoons chopped fresh basil |
| 4 tablespoons dry white wine | Salt and freshly ground black pepper |

Cook the pasta in a large pan of boiling salted water for 8 minutes or until *al dente*, then drain. Meanwhile, make the sauce. Heat the oil in a frying pan, add the bacon and fry for 5–7 minutes, adding the white wine half-way through the cooking time. Beat the egg yolks and cream together, then stir in the parsley and some salt and pepper. Add to the bacon and heat through gently without letting it boil.

To serve, pour the sauce over the drained pasta, mix well and sprinkle the basil over the top.

# MEAT DISHES

## ANTONY WORRALL THOMPSON

# BLACK PUDDING À LA FORESTIÈRE WITH PIEDMONTESE PEPPERS

*See photograph*

Janet Aitken from Berkshire has two passions, cooking and travel. Her ingredients were a mix of the exotic and the traditional and Antony gave homely black pudding a delicious Mediterranean twist with a dish of baked peppers.

**SERVES 2**

350 g (12 oz) potatoes, diced
75 g (3 oz) butter
1 tablespoon Greek yoghurt
5 small Cox's apples, peeled, cored and diced
Juice of 1 lemon
$1/_2$ onion, diced
2 bay leaves
1 teaspoon caster sugar
$1/_4$ teaspoon freshly grated nutmeg
1 teaspoon dried thyme

1 tablespoon olive oil
1 black pudding, sliced on the diagonal
Salt and freshly ground black pepper

**FOR THE PIEDMONTESE PEPPERS**
2 thin slices of onion
2 small tomatoes, cut in half and de-seeded
1 pepper, cut in half and de-seeded
$1/_2$ teaspoon dried thyme
1 tablespoon olive oil

Pre-heat the oven to gas mark 6, 200°C (400°F).

For the Piedmontese peppers, place 1 onion slice and 2 tomato halves in each pepper half, sprinkle with the thyme and then drizzle over the oil. Season with salt and pepper and bake in the oven for about 20 minutes, until the peppers are tender but not collapsed.

Meanwhile, cook the potatoes in boiling salted water until tender, then drain and mash with 25 g (1 oz) of the butter, the Greek yoghurt and seasoning to taste. Keep warm.

Put half the diced apple in a small bowl, pour over the lemon juice and leave for about 5 minutes, then drain.

73

Heat half the remaining butter in a small pan, add the onion and fry until softened and brown. Add the bay leaves, sugar and the lemon-soaked apple, season with salt and pepper and cook gently for 5 minutes, until the apple is tender.

Heat the remaining butter in a pan, add the nutmeg, thyme and remaining apple. Cook gently for 5 minutes, until the apple is tender and golden.

Heat the oil in a frying pan and gently fry the black pudding until it has been warmed through.

To serve, put the mashed potato on to 2 warmed serving plates and spoon the apple sauces next to it. Arrange the black pudding on top and accompany with the stuffed peppers.

## BRIAN TURNER

# POTIRON À LA FLAMANDE

Pumpkin stuffed with pork and apple in a cider sauce
*See photograph*

**Looking forward to a Hallowe'en celebration, Linda Walton from West London brought along a pumpkin and some pork. Brian turned the pork into a spooky special and served it inside the pumpkin.**

**SERVES 2**

| | |
|---|---|
| 1 small pumpkin, about 1 kg (2¼ lb) | ½ teaspoon paprika |
| 50 g (2 oz) butter | Salt and freshly ground black pepper |
| 2 tablespoons vegetable oil | |
| 2 eating apples, peeled, cored and finely diced | **FOR THE SAUCE** |
| 1 small onion, chopped | 300 ml (10 fl oz) chicken stock |
| 350 g (12 oz) potatoes, finely diced | 150 ml (5 fl oz) cider |
| 350 g (12 oz) pork loin steak, cut into | 150 ml (5 fl oz) double cream |
| 5 cm (2 inch) squares | 1 tablespoon Dijon mustard |

Pre-heat the oven to gas mark 6, 200°C (400°F).

Slice the top off the pumpkin and scoop out the seeds and most of the flesh, leaving a shell about 1 cm (¹/₂ inch) thick. Cut half the butter into small pieces and put them in the pumpkin shell. Place the pumpkin in an ovenproof dish and bake in the oven while you prepare the filling.

Heat the remaining butter and half the oil in a frying pan, add the apples, onion and potatoes and cook gently for about 10 minutes, until softened and golden brown. Season to taste. In a separate pan, heat the remaining oil, add the pork and paprika and fry for 8–10 minutes or until cooked through.

To make the sauce, put the stock and cider in a heavy-based pan and boil until reduced to half its original volume. Add the cream and simmer until reduced by almost half again, then stir in the mustard and season to taste.

To serve, stir the apple mixture and the pork into the sauce, then spoon the sauce into the pumpkin, arranging any extra around the pumpkin in the dish.

---

**READY STEADY COOK Tip**

*The pumpkin will not be cooked after so short a cooking time. If you have more time, bake it for about 40 minutes or until tender when pierced with a knife. The pumpkin flesh can be diced and cooked in boiling salted water, then stirred into the filling.*

---

## BRIAN TURNER

# AGNEAU AU FER À LA COMPOTE DES FRUITS

Lamb noisettes with fruit compote, runner beans and mint butter sauce

Pete Bowman from Birmingham enjoys lamb but only eats it as the Sunday roast. Brian showed him new ideas for his old favourite by combining it with a fruit compote.

**SERVES 2**

2 x 175 g (6 oz) lamb chump chops
1 tablespoon soy sauce
1 tablespoon runny honey
100 g (4 oz) runner beans, cut into 1 cm (1/2 inch) lengths
15 g (1/2 oz) butter
Salt and freshly ground black pepper

**FOR THE COMPOTE**

1 tablespoon olive oil
1/2 red onion, finely chopped

50 g (2 oz) ready-to-eat dried apricots, roughly chopped
50 g (2 oz) sultanas
125 g (4 oz) cranberries
150 ml (5 fl oz) dry white wine

**FOR THE SAUCE**

300 ml (10 fl oz) chicken stock
150 ml (5 fl oz) dry white wine
4 tablespoons brandy
75 g (3 oz) chilled butter, diced
1 tablespoon finely chopped fresh mint

Cut the lamb off the bone and trim off any excess fat, then tie into rounds (noisettes) with kitchen string (you could ask your butcher to do this). Place under a very hot grill for 1 minute on each side until browned. Put the soy sauce and honey in a small pan and heat gently for 1 minute, until slightly reduced and thickened. Brush this mixture all over the lamb and continue to cook for 4–6 minutes, until cooked and slightly caramelized on the outside and pink in the centre. Transfer to an ovenproof dish and keep warm in a low oven.

Meanwhile, make the compote. Heat the oil in a frying pan, add the onion and cook gently for a few minutes, until softened. Add the remaining ingredients and simmer for 10–15 minutes, until the fruit is soft and pulpy and most of the liquid has evaporated.

For the sauce, put the stock and white wine in a pan and boil for 5 minutes, then add the brandy and boil until the liquid is reduced to two-thirds of its original volume. Whisk in the butter a few pieces at a time, and boil until reduced to about 200 ml (7 fl oz). Stir in the mint and season to taste.

Cook the runner beans in a pan of boiling salted water for 3–4 minutes, until just tender, then drain. Melt the butter in a pan, toss the beans in it and season to taste.

To serve, pile the runner beans in the centre of each serving plate, place the lamb on top and surround with the fruit compote. Pour the sauce around the edge.

ANTONY WORRALL THOMPSON

# ALISON'S HOT AND SPICY DREAM

Steak with saffron rice and oyster mushroom stir-fry

Alison Hannigan from Rayleigh, Essex, had been given a wok but never had the courage to use it – or even get it out of the cupboard! With her favourite Chinese ingredients of beef, beansprouts, mushrooms and ginger, she challenged Antony to create a stir-fry that would inspire her to use the wok at home.

**SERVES 4**
175 g (6 oz) easy-cook long grain rice
A large pinch of saffron strands
1 tablespoon sunflower oil
350 g (12 oz) sirloin steak
1 tablespoon chopped fresh coriander

**FOR THE STIR-FRY**
1 chicken stock cube
175 g (6 oz) easy-cook long grain rice
100 g (4 oz) frozen peas
2 eggs
3 tablespoons sunflower oil
1 onion, finely chopped

3 garlic cloves, finely chopped
1 teaspoon ginger purée
$\frac{1}{2}$ teaspoon hot chilli powder
1 lemon grass stalk, finely chopped
85 ml (3 fl oz) water
100 g (4 oz) oyster mushrooms, sliced

100 g (4 oz) beansprouts
2 tablespoons soy sauce
2 tablespoons chopped fresh coriander
1 tablespoon chopped fresh parsley
Salt and freshly ground black pepper

First start preparing the stir-fry. Bring a pan of water to the boil, crumble in the stock cube and then add the rice. Simmer for 10–12 minutes or until the rice is just tender, adding the peas after about 8 minutes. Drain thoroughly and set aside.

Beat the eggs with 1 tablespoon of cold water and some seasoning. Heat 1 tablespoon of the oil in a 20 cm (8 inch) frying pan, pour in the eggs and cook, stirring the eggs and tilting the pan, to make an omelette. After 2–3 minutes, when the eggs are almost set, cook for a minute longer without stirring, then roll up the omelette, tip out on to a board and leave to cool.

Put the rice and saffron into a pan of boiling salted water and simmer for 10–12 minutes, until tender. Drain and keep warm.

Heat the oil in a griddle or a heavy-based frying pan until very hot. Add the steak and fry for 3–4 minutes on each side.

To finish the stir-fry, heat the remaining oil in a wok until very hot. Add the onion, garlic, ginger purée, chilli powder and lemon grass and stir-fry for 2 minutes. Add the water, then add the mushrooms and beansprouts and stir-fry for 1 minute. Stir in the white rice and peas with the soy sauce, coriander and parsley. Cut the rolled omelette into thin slices and add to the stir-fry.

To serve, spoon the saffron rice around the edge of a serving platter and sprinkle over the coriander. Fill the centre of the plate with the stir-fry. Slice the steak diagonally into strips and arrange on top.

---

### READY STEADY COOK Tip
*Reserve the ends from the onion and add one to each pan of rice for a little extra flavour.*

---

# DESSERTS

SEXY TOFFEE PUDDING AND
HEALTH ON A PLATE – 80

SAGITTARIAN PLUM TARTS WITH
GREEK YOGHURT – 82

CHOCOLATE MOUSSE – 83

ALI'S BIRTHDAY MONTAGE – 84

CARAMELIZED GROUND RICE PUDDINGS ON
A BED OF EXOTIC BANANA – 86

BAKED BANANAS WITH PINEAPPLE CARPACCIO
AND CARAMEL SAUCE – 87

FRUIT HEARTS – 89

PEARS WITH CRANBERRY COMPOTE AND
TWO-CHOCOLATE SAUCE – 90

# SEXY TOFFEE PUDDING AND HEALTH ON A PLATE

### Panettone and banana pudding with pink grapefruit and yoghurt salad

Rita Gordon from Denton, Manchester wanted Antony to make her the ultimate gooey pudding. She brought along a panettone, a reminder of a holiday in Italy with husband Keith.

| SERVES 6 | FOR THE PINK GRAPEFRUIT SALAD |
|---|---|
| 225 g (8 oz) butter | 1 pink grapefruit |
| 225 g (8 oz) light soft brown sugar | Juice of $1/_2$ orange |
| 8 tablespoons golden syrup | Grated rind of 1 orange |
| 5 ripe but firm bananas | 150 ml (5 fl oz) Greek yoghurt |
| 450 g (1 lb) panettone, cut horizontally into slices 2 cm ($3/_4$ inch) thick | 25 g (1 oz) caster sugar |
| | 1 tablespoon finely chopped fresh mint |
| 200 ml (7 fl oz) double cream | |
| 150 ml (5 fl oz) milk | |

First make the pink grapefruit salad. Peel the grapefruit, removing all the white pith, and cut out the segments from between the membranes. Squeeze the juice from the grapefruit membranes into a bowl and mix in the orange juice, half the orange rind, the yoghurt, caster sugar and mint. Spoon this mixture on to a serving plate and arrange the grapefruit segments on top, then sprinkle over the remaining orange rind.

Pre-heat the oven to gas mark 8, 230°C (450°F).

Divide the butter, brown sugar and golden syrup between 2 pans, one of which should be large enough to hold 2 whole bananas. Heat gently until the butter has melted and the sugar has dissolved, stirring now and again. Bring to the boil and simmer for about 3 minutes.

Peel the bananas and cut 3 of them into slices 1 cm ($\frac{1}{2}$ inch) thick. Add the sliced bananas to one of the pans of toffee sauce. Add the 2 remaining bananas to the other pan of toffee sauce. Continue to simmer both, stirring occasionally, for 3–4 minutes.

Use half the panettone slices to line the base of a 1.7 litre (3 pint) ovenproof dish, cutting them to fit. Put 150 ml (5 fl oz) of the cream in a pan with the milk and heat gently, then pour half of this mixture over the panettone. Spoon over the sliced banana sauce and cover with the remaining panettone. Pour over the remaining cream mixture and spoon over most of the toffee sauce from the second pan, reserving the whole bananas. Put the pudding in the oven for 5 minutes until it is heated through and caramelized on top. If necessary, place it under a hot grill to caramelize.

To serve, arrange the whole bananas on top of the panettone pudding and spoon over any remaining toffee sauce. Pour over the rest of the cream. Serve the pink grapefruit salad separately – or to anyone who is too fainthearted to tackle the pudding!

---

### READY STEADY COOK Tips
• *Panettone is a light Italian fruit bread, attractively packaged in boxes and available from delicatessens and supermarkets. If you cannot find one you could substitute brioche or a light fruit loaf.*
• *The pink grapefruit and yoghurt salad makes a refreshing breakfast dish – particularly if you have indulged in toffee pudding the night before!*
• *The toffee and sliced banana sauce makes a superb topping for ice-cream.*

---

## BRIAN TURNER

# SAGITTARIAN PLUM TARTS WITH GREEK YOGHURT

Ann Price from Stratford-upon-Avon is an astrology fan with a sweet tooth. In honour of her star sign, Brian made this fabulously fruity pudding, which tasted out of this world.

**SERVES 4**

175 g (6 oz) strawberry jam
50 g (2 oz) sultanas
100 g (4 oz) seedless black grapes, halved
4 tablespoons damson wine or red wine
A pinch of black pepper
4 tablespoons Greek yoghurt
250 ml (8 fl oz) double cream, lightly whipped
25 g (1 oz) butter

6 plums, halved and stoned
Caster sugar, to taste (optional)
Icing sugar, for dusting

**FOR THE PASTRY**

25 g (1 oz) ground almonds
225 g (8 oz) plain flour
100 g (4 oz) butter, diced
A pinch of salt
1 egg, beaten

Pre-heat the oven to gas mark 6, 200°C (400°F).

First make the pastry. Process the ground almonds, flour, butter and salt in a food processor until combined. Add the egg and process until the mixture just begins to bind together. Add a little cold water if necessary (no more than 1 tablespoon) and process just until the pastry forms a ball around the blade. Chill the pastry for at least 10 minutes, preferably half an hour. Roll out on a lightly floured surface until 5 mm ($^1/_4$ inch) thick and use to line four 10 cm (4 inch) tart tins. Cover each pastry case with a piece of crumpled greaseproof paper, weighed down with baking beans, and bake for 10 minutes. Remove the paper and baking beans and bake for a further 5 minutes, until the pastry is lightly browned. Remove from the oven and leave to cool on a wire rack.

Put the strawberry jam in a pan and heat, stirring occasionally, until melted. Set aside. Put the sultanas and grapes into a separate pan and heat gently for 1 minute, then add the wine and black pepper. Simmer for 3 minutes, until slightly reduced, then use a slotted spoon to transfer half the mixture to a bowl, draining it well. Leave to cool and then fold in the Greek yoghurt and 4 tablespoons of the whipped cream. Add the jam to the mixture in the pan and simmer until thickened, then remove from the heat and leave to cool.

Melt the butter in a pan, add the plum halves and cook gently for about 5 minutes, until tender. Taste and add a little sugar if necessary. Leave to cool.

Divide the fruit and yoghurt mixture between the pastry cases and place 3 plum halves on top of each one. Pipe the remaining cream on top of each tartlet.

To serve, place each tartlet on a serving plate and spoon the grape and jam compote around them. Dust with icing sugar.

A N T O N Y   W O R R A L L   T H O M P S O N

# CHOCOLATE MOUSSE

*See photograph*

### SERVES 2
100 g (4 oz) good-quality plain chocolate
2 eggs, separated
2 tablespoons double cream
2 tablespoons caster sugar

Break up the chocolate and melt it in a bowl set over a pan of simmering water (make sure the bowl is not touching the water). Remove from the heat and cool slightly, then beat in the egg yolks with a wooden spoon. Stir in the cream.

Whisk the egg whites until they form peaks, then add the sugar and continue to whisk until peaks form again. Using a metal spoon, gently fold the egg whites into the chocolate mixture, then spoon the mousse into individual moulds or dishes and chill for at least 30 minutes, preferably longer, until set.

B R I A N   T U R N E R

# ALI'S BIRTHDAY MONTAGE

As a special treat on her birthday, Ali Stevenson from Nottingham brought along some of her favourite fruits for a summer indulgence. She was delighted to be able to make something in 20 minutes – at home her two small daughters insist on 'mucking in' and everything takes twice as long!

**SERVES 4**
1 plum or peach, stoned and finely diced
1 mango, peeled, stoned and finely diced
50 g (2 oz) cherries, stoned and finely diced
100 g (4 oz) strawberries, sliced
caster sugar, to taste
150 ml (5 fl oz) double cream
icing sugar, for dusting

**FOR THE HAZELNUT BISCUITS**
75 g (3 oz) hazelnuts

75 g (3 oz) self-raising flour
75 g (3 oz) caster sugar
75 g (3 oz) butter
1 egg yolk, lightly beaten

**FOR THE STRAWBERRY COULIS**
225 g (8 oz) strawberries
25 g (1 oz) icing sugar, or to taste
1 tablespoon lemon juice, or to taste

Pre-heat the oven to gas mark 4, 180°C (350°F).

First make the biscuits. Process the hazelnuts finely in a food processor. Add the flour, sugar and butter and continue to process until the mixture resembles fine crumbs. Add the egg yolk and blend briefly. You may not need all the egg yolk; the mixture should just bind together but should not be wet. Form the dough into a log shape about 5 cm (2 inch) in diameter, wrap in greaseproof paper and chill in the freezer until firm.

Cut the biscuit dough into slices about 5 mm ($^1/_4$ inch) thick, place them well spaced out on a greased baking sheet and bake in the oven for 8–10 minutes, until pale golden. Transfer to a wire rack to cool.

For the strawberry coulis, blend the strawberries, icing sugar and lemon juice in a liquidizer until smooth. Pass the coulis through a sieve, then taste and add more icing sugar or lemon juice if necessary.

Mix together the plum or peach, mango, cherries and strawberries and sweeten to taste with caster sugar. Whip the cream until it forms soft peaks.

To serve, sift icing sugar over 4 of the biscuits and set aside. Place a biscuit on each serving plate, top with some of the fruit and then with a little whipped cream. Put another biscuit on top and repeat the fruit and cream layers, then top with the biscuits dusted with icing sugar. Pour the strawberry coulis around the biscuit stacks and serve.

---

### READY STEADY COOK Tips

- *You need 12 biscuits for this recipe so there will be some left over. Either bake all the biscuits and store the extra in an airtight tin, or cut 12 biscuits, then wrap the remaining dough and store in the freezer. When you want to make more biscuits it is very convenient simply to slice off what you need from the frozen dough.*
- *Any soft fruits can be used – try raspberries, blueberries, peaches, kiwi fruit, grapes or melon.*
- *Strawberry coulis goes well with ice-cream, fruit tarts and salads. It will keep in the refrigerator for 2 days and also freezes well.*

---

## BRIAN TURNER

# CARAMELIZED GROUND RICE PUDDINGS ON A BED OF EXOTIC BANANA

Betty Leigh, who runs a Blackpool B&B, gave Brian a real challenge when she brought along some ground rice. Undaunted, he turned it into a winning dish.

**SERVES 4**

**FOR THE PUDDINGS**
65 g (2¹/₂ oz) dried fruit, such as apricots, prunes and peaches, finely diced
450 ml (15 fl oz) milk
100 g (4 oz) ground rice
25 g (1 oz) caster sugar
300 ml (10 fl oz) double cream
2 egg yolks
50 g (2 oz) soft brown sugar

**FOR THE SAUCE**
3 oranges
75 g (3 oz) butter
75 g (3 oz) soft brown sugar
3 large bananas, diced
3–4 tablespoons rum, to taste
2 tablespoons honey
1 papaya, peeled, de-seeded and diced

Pre-heat the oven to gas mark 6, 200°C (400°F).

First make the ground rice puddings. Put the dried fruit into a small bowl, pour over hot water to cover and leave to soak for 5–10 minutes. Drain thoroughly and pat dry. Heat the milk in a pan until almost boiling, then add the ground rice, caster sugar and half the double cream. Bring to the boil, stirring continuously, and cook gently for 2 minutes, then whisk in the egg yolks. Remove from the heat and stir in the dried fruit, then spoon the mixture into 4 greased 7.5 cm (3 inch) ramekin dishes or individual brioche moulds. Place the dishes in a roasting tin containing 2.5 cm (1 inch) of water and bake in the oven for about 5 minutes, until set.

For the sauce, remove the rind from one of the oranges with a zester and set aside. Peel the oranges, removing all the white pith, and cut out the segments from between the membranes. Set aside. Melt 50 g (2 oz) of the butter and 50 g (2 oz) of the sugar in a frying pan, add the diced bananas and rum and let the mixture bubble for 1–2 minutes. Be careful not to overcook the bananas; they should retain their shape. Stir in the orange rind. In a separate pan, melt the remaining butter and sugar, stir in the orange segments and honey and cook until caramelized. Stir in the papaya and heat through gently.

Run a knife round the edge of each ground rice pudding to loosen it and turn out on to a baking tray or heatproof plate. Sprinkle the brown sugar over the top and place under a hot grill until caramelized. Whip the remaining cream until thick.

To serve, spoon the banana sauce into the centre of 4 serving plates and place the ground rice puddings on top. Arrange the caramelized oranges and papaya around the edges. Top the puddings with the whipped cream.

### ANTONY WORRALL THOMPSON

# BAKED BANANAS WITH PINEAPPLE CARPACCIO AND CARAMEL SAUCE

*See photograph*

The Tainsh family from Largs, Scotland, are known as the banana family at their local supermarket. True to form, Barbara brought along a bunch of bananas to challenge Antony – and learnt how to cut a pineapple.

| SERVES 4 | 85 ml (3 fl oz) double cream |
|---|---|
| 1 small pineapple | 1 teaspoon whisky, or to taste |
| 1 orange | 25 g (1 oz) good-quality plain |
| 1 lime | chocolate, grated |

| **FOR THE CARAMEL SAUCE** | **FOR THE BAKED BANANAS** |
|---|---|
| 100 g (4 oz) caster sugar | 4 bananas |
| 120 ml (4 fl oz) water | 75 g (3 oz) soft brown sugar |
| 200 ml (7 fl oz) double cream | 1 teaspoon cinnamon |
| | 25 g (1 oz) butter |
| | 2 tablespooons whisky |

Pre-heat the oven to gas mark 5, 190°C (375°F).

First make the caramel sauce. Put the sugar and water in a small pan and heat gently without stirring until dissolved. Bring to the boil and boil steadily for about 5 minutes, until it has turned a rich, golden caramel colour (watch it carefully to make sure it does not become too dark). Remove from the heat and pour in the cream, holding the pan well away from you in case it splatters. Return to the heat and cook gently, stirring, for 1–2 minutes, until the sauce is smooth. Do not let it boil again.

For the baked bananas, peel the bananas and place in a shallow ovenproof dish. Sprinkle over the brown sugar and cinnamon, dot with the butter and then pour over the whisky. Bake in the oven for 10–15 minutes, until softened.

Meanwhile, peel the pineapple, cut it into wafer-thin slices and arrange on a large serving platter. Peel the orange and lime, removing all the white pith, and cut out the segments from between the membranes. Arrange on top of the pineapple. Whip the cream until it forms peaks, then fold in the whisky.

To serve, place the baked bananas in the centre of the platter, on top of the pineapple, then top with the whipped cream and sprinkle over the grated chocolate. Serve with the caramel sauce.

---

### READY STEADY COOK Tip
*To peel the pineapple neatly, slice off all the skin, then remove the knots by making a small angled cut into the fruit on either side of a row of knots (the knots run in diagonal lines along the pineapple) and lifting them out.*

---

## A N T O N Y   W O R R A L L   T H O M P S O N

# FRUIT HEARTS
*See photograph*

Paul Morrison from Teddington, Middlesex, asked Antony to make a Valentine's Day dessert for his sweet-toothed wife, Kristen. Antony obliged with this romantic pudding and found time to make a chocolate mousse as well (see page 83). Meanwhile Kristen was cooking a special meal with Brian (see page 38).

| SERVES 2 | 2 passion fruit |
| --- | --- |
| 450 g (1 lb) puff pastry | Caster sugar, to taste |
| 1 egg yolk, beaten with 1 tablespoon water | 8 strawberries, sliced |
| 1 small mango | Icing sugar, for dusting |
| 150 ml (5 fl oz) double cream | |

Pre-heat the oven to gas mark 6, 200°C (400°F).

Cut the pastry in half and roll out each piece on a lightly floured surface to about 1 cm (½ inch) thick. With a sharp knife, cut out a heart shape from each piece of pastry, about 15 cm (6 inch) long. Place on a baking tray, brush with the beaten egg yolk and bake for about 15–20 minutes, until well risen and golden brown. Remove from the oven and leave on a wire rack until cool enough to handle, then cut each heart horizontally in half. If the pastry is not quite cooked through, return the hearts to the oven, cut-side up, for a few minutes. Leave on a wire rack to cool completely.

Meanwhile, peel the mango and cut the flesh away from the stone. Cut a few long slices for decoration and dice the remaining flesh. Set aside.

Whip the cream until thick. Cut the passion fruit in half and use a teaspoon to scoop out the seeds and flesh. Fold them gently into the whipped cream and sweeten to taste with caster sugar.

To serve, place the bottom half of each pastry heart on a serving plate and spread the passion fruit cream over it. Cover the cream with the diced mango and strawberries and top with the remaining pastry half. Dust the fruit hearts with icing sugar and decorate with the reserved mango slices.

---

### READY STEADY COOK Tip
*To make 2 pastry hearts exactly the same size, cut out one heart, then place it on the other piece of pastry and cut round it. Alternatively you could use a cardboard template.*

---

BRIAN TURNER

# PEARS WITH CRANBERRY COMPOTE AND TWO-CHOCOLATE SAUCE

*See photograph*

Stephanie Bayliss from Beckenham, Kent, confessed to having a very sweet tooth. She brought along two types of chocolate and some fruit and Brian put together this luxurious dessert.

| SERVES 2 | FOR THE COMPOTE |
|---|---|
| 2 pears | 25 g (1 oz) butter |
| Juice of $1/2$ lemon | 50 g (2 oz) caster sugar |
| Grated rind of 1 orange | 225 g (8 oz) cranberries |
| 25 g (1 oz) butter | Juice of $1/2$ orange |
| A little caster sugar, for sprinkling | **FOR THE CHOCOLATE SAUCE** |
| 2 ginger nut biscuits, crushed | 150 ml (5 fl oz) double cream |
| 1 tablespoon flaked almonds, toasted | 75 g (3 oz) good-quality plain chocolate |
| Icing sugar, for dusting | 15 g ($1/2$ oz) butter |
| | 25 g (1 oz) white chocolate drops |

First make the cranberry compote. Melt the butter and sugar in a frying pan, add the cranberries and orange juice and simmer for 2 minutes or until softened. Keep warm.

Peel, halve and core the pears, then put them into a bowl of water with the lemon juice to prevent them browning.

Bring a pan of water to the boil, add the orange rind and simmer for 1–2 minutes. Remove with a slotted spoon, refresh in cold water and pat dry. Reserve for decoration. Add the pear halves to the pan and poach for about 5 minutes or until just tender. Drain the pear halves, then place them on a board, cut-side down, and slice thinly, leaving them joined at the top. Press down lightly on each pear half with the palm of your hand to make a fan shape. Melt the butter in a frying pan and, using a fish slice, carefully transfer the pears to it, rounded-side down. Fry until golden, then turn over to cook the other side. Sprinkle with a little caster sugar and place under a hot grill until lightly caramelized. Keep warm.

To make the chocolate sauce, bring the double cream to the boil in a pan, then gradually add chunks of the plain chocolate, whisking until smooth. Remove from the heat and whisk in the butter to give a glossy finish.

To serve, spoon the cranberry compote into the centre of 2 large serving plates and arrange the pears on top. Sprinkle with the orange rind and the crushed ginger nut biscuits. Pour the hot chocolate sauce around and dot the white chocolate drops all over it – they will melt into the sauce. Finally sprinkle over the flaked almonds and dust with icing sugar.

---

### READY STEADY COOK Tip

*This is delicious but extremely rich. For a simpler dessert, just serve the pears on the cranberry compote, sprinkled with the flaked almonds and dusted with icing sugar. You could just poach the pears, omitting the caramelizing. The chocolate sauce is very good with ice-cream.*

---

# INDEX

## A

apples
  pumpkin stuffed with pork and
    apple in a cider sauce 74–5
  spicy mackerel fillets on tasty
    Tenby treats 27–8
asparagus 38–9
aubergines 14
  and tomato sauce 10

## B

bacon
  bacon–wrapped tomatoes 57–8
  fried kidneys and bacon on carrot
    purée with mushroom and
    coriander sauce 62–3
bananas
  baked with pineapple carpaccio
    and caramel sauce 87–8
  banana sauce 86–7
  deep–fried 47–8
  panettone and banana pudding
    80–1
beans see green beans; haricot
  beans; runner beans
beef
  jet–lag steak stack 63–4
  meatballs with couscous,
    vegetables and mint and
    yoghurt sauce 65–6
  spaghetti bolognese 70
  spicy steak with warm mushroom

salad and hollandaise sauce
    59–60
  steak and ratatouille with polenta
    and grilled vegetables 67–8
  steak with saffon rice and oyster
    mushroom stir–fry 77–8
biscuits, hazelnut 84–5
black pudding à la forestière with
  Piedmontese peppers 73–4
brandy cream sauce 22–3
brioche, baked filled with pork and
  sage patties, mushrooms, bacon–
  wrapped tomatoes, fried eggs
  and fried onion rings 57–8
bruschetta with olive paste,
  aubergine and Mozzarella 14
bubble and squeak, Yorkshire 42–3

## C

cabbage 69
  parcels 16–7
caramel sauce 87–8
carrots
  and leek garnish 29–30
  purée 62–3
  rösti 43–4
celeriac, roasted 49–50
cheeses see red Leicester;
  Mozzarella; ricotta
chick pea salad 54–5
chicken
  Atlanta with kumquat chutney and
    asparagus 38–9
  breasts and tomatoes stuffed with

# INDEX

ricotta and pesto, served with sauce vierge 40–1

cooked in two ways with carrot rösti, sautéed vegetables and tarragon cream sauce 43–4

deep–fried with chicken and pineapple fricassée 47–8

fried on a bed of courgettes and peppers with marmalade sauce 35–6

honey and lime with roasted celeriac, chicken liver mousse and mushroom sauce 49–50

on a potato galette with green beans and lemon butter herb sauce 45–6

spicy with saffron rice, seafood and stuffed tomatoes 33–4

spinach–stuffed leg on turmeric–braised potatoes with cumin–fried onions 36–7

stuffed breasts with mixed vegetables and mead sauce 32–3

chicory, braised 25–6

chocolate
mousse 83–4
two–chocolate sauce 90–1

cider sauce 74–5

cod, battered with deep–fried potato balls and cabbage parcels16–17

courgettes 35–6
ribbons 24–5

couscous
meatballs with 65–6
salad 54–5

cranberry compote 90–1

cucumber and yoghurt soup 40–1

## F

farfalle carbonara 72

fennel 20–1

fish see cod; mackerel; plaice; salmon; shellfish; trout

fruit
Ali's birthday montage 84–5
compote 76–7
hearts 89
see also individual fruit e.g. bananas

fusilli with aubergine and tomato sauce 10

## G

game see pheasant

grapefruit and yoghurt salad 80–1

green beans 45–6
salad 63–4

guacamole 25–6

## H

ham with hot pineapple chutney 55–6

haricot beans, stew 51–2

hazelnut biscuits 84–5

93

# INDEX

# READY
# STEADY
# COOK
# 2

# READY
# STEADY
# COOK
# 2

RICHARD CAWLEY

PATRICK ANTHONY

PHOTOGRAPHS BY
JULIET PIDDINGTON

**BBC BOOKS**

This book is published to accompany the television series *Ready Steady Cook*
which was first broadcast in Autumn 1994.
The series was produced by Bazal Productions.

Published by BBC Books, an imprint of BBC Worldwide Publishing,
BBC Worldwide Ltd, Woodlands, 80 Wood Lane, London W12 0TT

First published 1996
Format © Bazal Productions
Recipes © Richard Cawley and Patrick Anthony
The moral right of the authors has been asserted.

Photographs: Juliet Piddington
Home Economist: Emma Patmore
ISBN 0 563 38757 2

Set in Futura
Designed by Louise Morley
Printed Martins the Printers Ltd, Berwick-upon-Tweed
Bound by Hunter & Foulis Ltd, Edinburgh
Colour separation by Radstock Reproductions Ltd, Midsomer Norton
Cover printed by Clays Ltd, St Ives plc

# CONTENTS

# INTRODUCTION

After the phenomenal success of the first *Ready Steady Cook* book, there simply had to be a follow-up, so now there are many more delicious recipes for you to prepare. If you have ever started one of our recipes, fired with enthusiasm after the show, only to find you can't remember quite how it finished, this is the book for you.

On *Ready Steady Cook* we give our chefs the ultimate culinary test. The budget is £5, the time limit is 20 minutes and, on top of all that, the ingredients are a complete surprise. Our contestants have chosen a combination of foods they love and it's the chef's job to invent a delicious recipe there and then.

These recipes make it possible for anyone to rustle up a gourmet dish. The book is full of new ideas (even the chefs surprise themselves sometimes) and it's guaranteed to inspire good and bad cooks alike.

The point is have a go – cooking is fun and the eating is even better! You can knock up a fabulous dish in 20 minutes for a fiver. Honestly. Go on – give it a try.

*Fern Britton*

x

Presenter, *Ready Steady Cook*

# A Note on Ingredients and Techniques

Good-quality ingredients make all the difference to the taste of the finished dish. For best results, choose unsalted butter and extra virgin olive oil. Buy ripe, flavoursome tomatoes, whenever possible, and really fresh herbs. If a recipe specifies dried herbs, freeze-dried ones usually have the best flavour. For desserts, chocolate should contain at least 50 per cent cocoa solids – check the back of the wrapper.

> Some of the recipes contain raw or lightly cooked eggs. Because of the slight risk of salmonella poisoning, these should be avoided by the sick, the elderly, the very young, and pregnant women.
> The chances of contamination are greatly reduced if you buy free-range eggs, preferably organic, from a reputable supplier.

Many of the recipes in this book include wine. Use a wine that you would enjoy drinking rather than cheap 'cooking' wine – if it's not worth drinking, it's not worth cooking with!

A technique favoured by the chefs on *Ready Steady Cook* is cooking on a ridged grill pan. Ridged grill pans are made of cast iron and usually have a spout for pouring off the cooking juices. They are a very healthy way of cooking because the ridges keep the food raised above any fat that runs off. They also make attractive grill marks on food – to make a criss-cross pattern, give the food a half-turn half-way through cooking each side. Use ridged grill pans for steaks, chops, fish or chunky slices of vegetables such as aubergines, courgettes or peppers.

Finally, *Ready Steady Cook* is all about putting together a delicious meal from whatever ingredients you have to hand. The recipes in this book are proof that some of the most memorable dishes are the ones that come about on the spur of the moment. So, if you don't have a particular ingredient, follow the example of our chefs and improvise. Don't be afraid to get in the kitchen and *Ready Steady Cook*!

## LARDER INGREDIENTS USED ON
## *READY STEADY COOK*

Arrowroot
Baking powder
Balsamic vinegar
Beef stock cubes
Black syrup
Bottle of red wine
Bottle of white wine
Cardamom pods
Caster sugar
Cayenne pepper
Chicken stock cubes
Cornflour
Demerara sugar
Dijon mustard
Double cream
Dried mixed herbs
Dried oregano
Eggs, size 3
Fresh basil
Fresh coriander
Fresh dill
Fresh parsley
Fresh rosemary
Fresh sage
Fresh thyme
Fresh white bread
Garam masala
Garlic
Granulated sugar

Golden syrup
Greek yoghurt
Ground all-spice
Ground cinnamon
Ground coriander
Ground ginger
Lemons/Limes
Mayonnaise
Milk
Mustard seeds
Olive oil
Oranges
Plain flour
Poppy seeds
Red wine vinegar
Self-raising flour
Sesame oil
Soft brown sugar
Soy sauce
Sunflower oil
Tabasco sauce
Tomato purée
Tomato sauce
Turmeric
Unsalted butter
Vanilla essence
Vegetable stock cubes
White wine vinegar
Wholegrain mustard

# VEGETARIAN DISHES

RACHEL'S DELECTABLE THAI DREAM – 10

HAVE YOURSELF A VEGGIE LITTLE CHRISTMAS – 12

RAQUEL'S RAVISHING MUSHROOM TART – 14

DANIELLE'S CAULIFLOWER CHARMER – 15

BARBARA'S FILO DREAMBOATS – 17

MICHELLE'S MÉLANGE – 19

WENDY'S WINTER WONDER – 20

FRANCES'S FAST FEAST – 22

## RICHARD CAWLEY

# RACHEL'S DELECTABLE THAI DREAM

Raw and cooked vegetables, with crisp-fried and soft noodles

Rachel Morton, of Reading, is a great fan of ethnic food, from Mexican to Chinese, but she had never tasted Thai food. She asked Richard to make an authentic Thai dish with the ingredients she brought and he obliged with this beautifully balanced recipe of raw and cooked vegetables and crisp and soft noodles. The coconut and lime flavouring of the stir-fry is the essence of Thai cooking.

| | |
|---|---|
| **SERVES 2** | 100 g (4 oz) green beans, trimmed |
| 4 carrots | 1 garlic clove, crushed |
| 4 spring onions | 1 fresh red chilli, seeded and chopped |
| 1 red pepper, halved and seeded | 1 teaspoon ground ginger |
| 100 g (4 oz) broccoli | 200 ml (7 fl oz) coconut cream |
| 4 tablespoons sunflower oil | Juice of I lime |
| 1 tablespoon white-wine vinegar | 225 g (8 oz) soft Chinese-style noodles |
| 1 teaspoon sesame oil | Sunflower oil for deep-frying |
| 1 teaspoon plus 1 tablespoon soy sauce | Salt and freshly ground black pepper |
| 1 tablespoon sesame seeds | Chopped fresh mint and coriander, to garnish |

Cut two carrots, two spring onions, half the red pepper and half of the stalk of the broccoli into thin matchsticks. Mix 2 tablespoons of the sunflower oil, the vinegar, sesame oil, the teaspoon of soy sauce and salt and pepper to taste. Put the mixed vegetable strips in a bowl, add the dressing and toss together. Dry-fry the sesame seeds in a small frying-pan for 1–2 minutes, until golden; then set aside.

Diagonally slice the remaining carrots. Chop the rest of the red pepper and slice the rest of the stalk of the broccoli. Cut the rest of the broccoli into small florets. Heat a tablespoon of sunflower oil in a wok, add the sliced carrots, broccoli stalks and florets, red pepper, green beans, garlic and chilli and stir-fry for 3 minutes. Add the ginger and cook for a minute. Add the tablespoon of soy sauce, the coconut cream and lime juice and cook for 3 minutes more.

Heat the oil to 190°C (375°F). Then add a quarter of the noodles and deep-fry them for 30 seconds, until crisp. Drain on absorbent kitchen paper.

Diagonally slice the remaining two spring onions. Heat a tablespoon of sunflower oil in a wok, add the spring onions and cook for a minute. Add the rest of the noodles and cook for 2 minutes.

To serve, pile the spring onions and noodles on a serving plate and spoon over the stir-fried vegetables. Arrange the deep-fried noodles on top of the mixed vegetable salad. Sprinkle the toasted sesame seeds and chopped mint and coriander over the stir-fry and the salad, to garnish.

---

### READY STEADY COOK Tips

• *If you don't have a thermometer or a deep-fryer, check that the oil is hot enough for deep-frying the noodles by throwing in a cube of day-old bread: it should brown in 30 seconds.*

• *One way to perfect stir-fries, as always, is to cut the vegetables into pieces that are roughly the same size, so they cook in about the same time.*

• *Precise cooking times and attention to what's happening in the wok are vital for all kinds of stir-frying. Make sure you prepare as much as possible before you begin cooking, so you can give the cooking your full attention.*

---

## RICHARD CAWLEY

# HAVE YOURSELF A VEGGIE LITTLE CHRISTMAS

Chestnut and cranberry pudding and orange salad, with garlic mushrooms on toast

Harriet Olaleye, from London, wanted a new idea for a vegetarian Christmas dinner, using the traditional Christmas ingredients of chestnuts and cranberries. Richard obliged with this traditional-style suet pudding.

**SERVES 2 UNACCOMPANIED AND 4 WITH EXTRA VEGETABLES**

**FOR THE PUDDING**

225 g (8 oz) self-raising flour
100 g (4 oz) vegetable suet
½ teaspoon dried oregano
2 tablespoons sunflower oil
1 large onion, chopped
240 g (8½ oz) tin of peeled chestnuts, roughly chopped
1 dessert apple, peeled, cored and chopped
225 g (8 oz) fresh or defrosted frozen cranberries
1 tablespoon chopped fresh sage
75 ml (3 fl oz) red wine
50 ml (2 fl oz) water
Salt and freshly ground black pepper

**FOR THE GARLIC MUSHROOMS**

25 g (1 oz) butter
1 tablespoon olive oil
225 g (8 oz) button mushrooms, quartered
2 garlic cloves, crushed
150 ml (5 fl oz) double cream
1 tablespoon chopped fresh parsley
4 slices of bread

**FOR THE ORANGE SALAD**

1 teaspoon lemon juice
1 tablespoon olive oil
2 tablespoons snipped fresh chives
2 oranges, peeled and segmented
Snipped fresh chives, to garnish

Mix the flour, suet, oregano and seasoning in a bowl. Stir in enough cold water, a little at a time, to make a smooth, firm dough. Turn out on to a lightly floured surface, knead gently and roll out to a circle

measuring about 30 cm (12 in) in diameter and 5 mm (¼ in) thick.
Cut out one quarter of the circle and set it aside for the lid. Use the
remaining three-quarters of the pastry to line an oiled 1.2 litre (2 pint)
pudding basin or microwave-proof glass bowl. Bring the cut edges
together to form a cone shape. Press the join together.

Heat 2 tablespoons of oil in a pan, add the onion and cook for
5 minutes, stirring occasionally. Put two-thirds of the onion in a bowl,
with the chestnuts, apple, half of the cranberries, the sage and
seasoning; mix well. Spoon into the pastry case and pour in the wine
and water. Roll the reserved piece of pastry to make a lid for the
pudding. Brush the edge of the lid with water, put the pastry lid on
and smooth the seam to seal the pudding; trim the top edges. Cover
with cling film and cook in the microwave on full power for
10 minutes.

For the garlic mushrooms, melt the butter and olive oil in a frying-
pan, add the button mushrooms and cook for 3 minutes. Add the
garlic, half of the reserved onion, the rest of the cranberries, the
cream, parsley and seasoning and cook for 2 minutes. Toast the slices
of bread, until golden.

To make the orange salad, mix the lemon juice, oil, chives and
seasoning. Add the orange segments and the rest of the onion and
toss together.

To serve, spoon the garlic mushrooms over the toast and garnish
with fresh chives. Serve the chestnut and cranberry pudding with the
orange salad.

---

### READY STEADY COOK Tip

• *You can still have Chirstmas dinner with a traditional feel, even
though it is vegetarian, if you use the classic Christmas ingredients
(except the turkey) in imaginative ways. Consider making chestnut
or sage and onion stuffing balls and serving little vegetarian
sausages, for example.*

RICHARD CAWLEY

# RAQUEL'S RAVISHING MUSHROOM TART

Raquel Addleman, from Bury, Lancashire, is one of twins. She and her sister wear the same clothes and live in the same road and their babies were born within hours of each other. Raquel had never cooked with filo pastry and sun-dried tomatoes, so she asked Richard to show her how to use them to advantage.

| SERVES 2 | Juice of ½ lemon |
|---|---|
| 25 g (1 oz) butter, melted | 1 tablespoon French mustard |
| 5 sheets of filo pastry, halved | 5 sun-dried tomato halves in oil, sliced |
| 2 eggs | 1 teaspoon caster sugar |
| 1 tablespoon olive oil | ½ frisée lettuce |
| 100 g (4 oz) mushrooms, sliced | Salt and freshly ground black pepper |
| 2 garlic cloves, chopped | 1 tablespoon grated parmesan, to serve |
| 3 tablespoons chopped fresh parsley | |

Pre-heat the oven to gas mark 6, 200°C (400°F). Butter two 10 cm (4 in) round flan cases or tartlet tins and line each with 4–5 layers of filo, brushing each layer with melted butter. Trim the edges. Place the pastry cases on a baking sheet and bake in the preheated oven for 8–10 minutes.

To poach the eggs, firstly, fill a bowl with boiling water. Put the two raw eggs (still in their shells) in the bowl and leave for 60 seconds. Remove the eggs and break them into a pan of boiling water. Cook the eggs for 2–3 minutes; they should stay in perfect shape. (You can cook the eggs ahead of time and keep them in a bowl of cold water. To reheat them, return them to boiling water for a minute.)

Sauté the mushrooms in the olive oil. Season and add half the garlic. Cook for 5 minutes. Then add the parsley and cook for a further 2 minutes.

To make the salad dressing, mix together 2 tablespoons of oil from the sun-dried tomatoes (or olive oil), the lemon juice, mustard, the remaining garlic, the sun-dried tomatoes and caster sugar. Toss the lettuce in the dressing.

To serve, spoon the mushrooms into the filo pastry cases and top each with a poached egg. Sprinkle the parmesan on top and serve with the salad.

PATRICK ANTHONY

# DANIELLE'S CAULIFLOWER CHARMER

Cauliflower and root vegetables in a creamy curry sauce

*A health-conscious student of dance and drama, Danielle Campbell-Scott brought along her favourite vegetarian ingredients. Patrick concocted a delicious curry: root vegetables take wonderfully well to being cooked with spices, because they absorb the flavours beautifully. Serve this with plain boiled rice for a vegetarian main course.*

**SERVES 2**

350 g (12 oz) sweet potato, peeled and cubed
1 potato, peeled and cubed
1 teaspoon paprika
½ cauliflower, cut in florets
1 tablespoon sunflower oil
25 g (1 oz) butter
½ onion, finely chopped
½ fresh green chilli, seeded and finely chopped
1 teaspoon ground turmeric
1 teaspoon garam masala
1 teaspoon ground coriander
1 teaspoon ground cumin
½ green pepper, seeded and chopped
2 tablespoons natural yoghurt
1 egg yolk

**TO SERVE**

1 banana, sliced
Lemon juice
Sprigs of coriander or parsley (optional), to garnish

Cook the sweet potato and potato in lightly salted, boiling water for 15 minutes. Drain them and sprinkle over the paprika. Meanwhile, steam the cauliflower for 10 minutes.

For the curry sauce, heat the oil and butter, fry the onion and chilli for 2–3 minutes until softened. Add the turmeric, garam masala, coriander, cumin and 6 tablespoons of water. Season and cook for 5 minutes. Add the green pepper and cook for a further 10 minutes.

Meanwhile, mix the yoghurt and egg yolk together in a small bowl. (The yolk will stop the yoghurt from curdling when it is cooked.) Stir the yoghurt and egg mix into the curry sauce and continue to cook the sauce for 3 minutes.

Slice the banana and squeeze some lemon juice over it, to stop it from discolouring.

To serve, place the cauliflower in the centre of a plate and surround it with the potatoes. Pour over the curry sauce and garnish with coriander or parsley, if you like. Serve the banana slices as an accompaniment.

---

### READY STEADY COOK Tips

• *Make sure the sauce doesn't boil after you add the yoghurt and egg yolk mixture: although the egg yolk will stop the yoghurt from curdling, if the heat is too high the yolk will go grainy.*

• *Other kinds of fruit can be served as a refreshing accompaniment to all kinds of curries and spicy dishes. Even ordinary sliced apples and oranges, perhaps with a few raisins and a little desiccated coconut, can make a meal more special, or splash out on more exotic tropical fruit like mangoes.*

## PATRICK ANTHONY

# BARBARA'S FILO DREAMBOATS

Filo pastry 'boats' with two vegetable fillings

Patrick was asked to create a really delectable vegetarian idea by Barbara Roll, from Abridge, Essex, who wants to avoid eating red meat and fish. Half the filo containers are filled with a delicious and fragrant mixture of chestnut mushrooms and aubergines; the others with a rich and piquant courgette and tomato filling.

**SERVES 2**
25 g (1 oz) butter, melted
6 sheets of filo pastry

**FOR THE AUBERGINE FILLING**
1 tablespoon sunflower oil
1 tablespoon olive oil
½ aubergine, cut in 1 cm (½ in) cubes
100 g (4 oz) chestnut mushrooms, roughly chopped
1 teaspoon lemon-grass paste

**FOR THE COURGETTE FILLING**
1 tablespoon sunflower oil
1 small courgette, cubed
½ red onion, chopped

3 tomatoes, skinned and chopped
1 teaspoon caster sugar
1 teaspoon tomato purée
½ teaspoon Dijon mustard
½ teaspoon balsamic vinegar
Salt and freshly ground black pepper

**TO SERVE**
4 tablespoons double cream
A few drops of sesame oil
A few drops of Tabasco sauce
4 tablespoons Greek yoghurt
1 tablespoon chopped fresh flatleaf parsley
1 tablespoon chopped fresh basil
Sprigs of flatleaf parsley and strips of courgette skin, to garnish

Pre-heat the oven to gas mark 6, 200°C (400°F). Put four upturned ramekin dishes on a baking tray and brush them with melted butter. Cut six sheets of filo pastry in half, brush each with melted butter and layer three pieces loosely over each ramekin dish. Trim if necessary. Bake in the oven for 10–12 minutes, until golden and crisp.

Heat the sunflower and olive oils in a frying-pan, add the aubergine and mushrooms and season well with black pepper. Cook for 3 minutes, stirring occasionally. Add the lemon-grass paste and cook for another 3 minutes. For the courgette filling, heat the oil in another frying-pan, add the courgette, onion, tomatoes, sugar, tomato purée and seasoning and cook for 5 minutes, stirring occasionally. Stir in the mustard and vinegar.

Take the filo baskets off the ramekin dishes and put them on the baking tray. Spoon each of the vegetable mixtures into two baskets and drizzle a tablespoon of cream over each of the courgette baskets. Return to the oven for 3 minutes.

Drizzle a few drops of sesame oil and Tabasco sauce over one side of each serving plate and put the aubergine basket on top. Spoon the Greek yoghurt on top of the aubergine mixture. Drizzle a tablespoon of cream over the other side of each serving plate and put the courgette baskets on top. Sprinkle the chopped herbs over both baskets and garnish with sprigs of parsley and strips of courgette skin.

---

### READY STEADY COOK Tips

• *Filo pastry dries out very quickly and becomes brittle and hard to handle. To prevent this, put the sheets you are not working with under a clean, slightly damp tea towel.*

• *This dish would also be delicious with more unusual kinds of mushrooms, such as oyster, shiitake or even fresh wild mushrooms, if you can get them.*

---

## PATRICK ANTHONY

# MICHELLE'S MÉLANGE

Red and green gratin, with deep-fried artichoke 'crisps'

Busy vegetarian mother-of-two Michelle Wells, from Peterborough, brought along her family's favourite vegetables, with some Jerusalem artichokes, which she had never tried to cook. Patrick peeled them into ribbons and deep-fried them to make delicious home-made 'crisps' to serve as a crunchy garnish to this tasty gratin.

**SERVES 4 AS A MAIN COURSE, 6 AS AN ACCOMPANIMENT**
450 g (1 lb) greens, shredded
450 g (1 lb) broccoli, cut in florets
2 beef tomatoes

**FOR THE CHEESE SAUCE**
25 g (1 oz) butter
25 g (1 oz) plain flour
300 ml (10 fl oz) milk

100 g (4 oz) Cheddar cheese, half diced, half grated

**FOR THE ARTICHOKE CRISPS**
Sunflower oil, for deep-frying
225 g (8 oz) Jerusalem artichokes, peeled

**TO GARNISH**
1 tablespoon chopped fresh parsley
Bunches of fresh herbs (optional)

In a two-tier steamer, place the greens in the bottom section and steam for 8 minutes. Add the broccoli to the top section and steam for 6 minutes. (Or you could cook the vegetables in lightly salted, boiling water.) Drain the vegetables and place in a casserole dish.

Meanwhile, halve the tomatoes and put them under a hot grill for 5 minutes, until they are partially cooked. Remove from the grill. Remove the skins, chop the flesh and add to the vegetables.

For the all-in-one cheese sauce, put the butter, flour and milk in a pan, bring to the boil, whisking continuously and simmer for 2 minutes until thickened. Remove from the heat, add the diced cheese and mix well as the cheese melts. When smooth and blended, pour the cheese sauce over the vegetables. Sprinkle the grated cheese over and put the dish under a hot grill for 3 minutes, or until the cheese has melted and browned slightly.

Heat the oil for deep-frying in a small pan. Cut the artichokes into thin ribbons with a potato peeler. Deep-fry the ribbons of artichoke until crisp and golden brown. Drain on kitchen paper.

To serve, sprinkle the artichoke crisps on top of the vegetables and around the edge. Garnish with chopped parsley and bunches of fresh herbs, if you like.

## PATRICK ANTHONY

# WENDY'S WINTER WONDER

### Stuffed mushrooms, with sautéed aubergine and cheese sauce

In a programme broadcast in the depth of winter's cold, Wendy Burnley, from Scarborough, asked Patrick to come up with an idea for a warming vegetarian dish that would be tasty enough to serve to her sister when she comes to visit. This delicious stuffed-mushroom recipe perfectly fits the bill.

**SERVES 2 AS A MAIN COURSE, 4 AS A STARTER**

4 large mushrooms, stalks removed and chopped finely
4 tablespoons olive oil, plus a little extra
100 g (4 oz) white rice
½ onion, finely chopped
1 garlic clove, chopped
4 fresh basil leaves, chopped
4 tablespoons tinned chopped tomatoes
½ aubergine, cubed
Salt and freshly ground black pepper

**FOR THE CHEESE SAUCE**
25 g (1 oz) butter
25 g (1 oz) plain flour
300 ml (10 fl oz) milk
60 g (2½ oz) Cheddar cheese, cubed
1 tablespoon double cream

Pre-heat the oven to gas mark 6, 200°C (400°F). Brush the mushroom caps with a little oil and put them in a lightly greased casserole dish. Bake in the oven for 12–15 minutes.

Bring some water to the boil and add salt. Add the rice and boil for 12 minutes. Drain the rice.

Heat a tablespoon of oil in a frying-pan, add the onion, garlic and basil, season and fry until softened, stirring occasionally. Add the tomatoes and the chopped mushroom stalks. Cook for a further 2 minutes. Add the cooked rice to the onion and tomato sauce, mix thoroughly and take off the heat.

Heat the remaining oil in a frying-pan, add the aubergine and stir-fry for 3–4 minutes. Season well.

Whisk together the butter, flour and milk in a pan over a low heat until smooth and well blended. When the sauce has thickened, add the cheese and double cream and continue to heat gently, whisking constantly, for 2 minutes.

To serve, put the mushrooms on a plate, spoon some of the rice filling into each, surround with the aubergine and pour the cheese sauce over the top.

---

### READY STEADY COOK Tips

• *If you want to serve this as a vegetarian main course, just add some fresh vegetables for colour and texture: the stuffed mushrooms are substantial enough for a meal in themselves and the rice in the filling means you don't need any other carbohydrate.*

• *You could also serve the mushrooms with a well-flavoured tomato sauce, perhaps sprinkled with a little grated cheese and browned under a hot grill for a few moments.*

## RICHARD CAWLEY

# FRANCES'S FAST FEAST

### Super-quick cheese soufflés, with chicory and avocado salad

Frances Lynch Smith, from Coventry, has been a vegetarian since she was in her early teens. She asked Richard to show her the quickest way to make soufflés that would be an instant hit at dinner parties. Richard served the rich soufflés with a refreshingly crisp salad in which slightly bitter chicory leaves are complemented by creamy avocado.

**SERVES 2**

**FOR THE SOUFFLÉS**
50 g (2 oz) butter
150 ml (5 fl oz) milk
25 g (1 oz) plain flour
2 eggs, separated
50 g (2 oz) Cheddar or Gruyère cheese, grated
2–3 drops of Tabasco sauce

½ teaspoon cayenne pepper
Salt and freshly ground black pepper
Fresh parsley sprigs, to garnish

**FOR THE SALAD**
1 avocado, stoned and mashed
1 tomato, chopped
2 tablespoons roughly chopped fresh coriander
½ onion, chopped
6 chicory leaves

For the soufflés: pre-heat the oven to gas mark 6, 200°C (400°F). Melt half of the butter and use it to grease two ramekins.

Make a white sauce by mixing the flour, milk and remaining butter in a pan. Bring to the boil, whisking continuously. Simmer for 2 minutes to thicken the sauce. Remove from the heat. Add the egg yolks, cheese, Tabasco, cayenne and seasoning and stir vigorously.

Whisk the egg whites until stiff. Fold a third into the cheese mixture with a metal spoon, then add the remainder. Pour the mixture into the ramekins and bake for 12–14 minutes, until well risen.

Mix the avocado, tomato, coriander and onion well and season. Separate the chicory leaves. Spoon a tablespoon of the avocado mixture on to each chicory leaf. Put the stuffed chicory leaves on a plate, in a star shape. Serve the soufflés separately, and garnish.

# FISH DISHES

## PATRICK ANTHONY

# MANDY'S SALMON MARVEL

Seared salmon steaks with vegetables, cucumber salad
and herb mayonnaise

Mandy Lee, from Blackpool, loves fish but is married to a fish-hater. She brought salmon
steaks to the programme and wanted a really special recipe as a treat for herself.

**SERVES 2**
2 salmon steaks
Sunflower oil
225 g (8 oz) new potatoes, lightly scraped
1 leek, sliced in thin strips
1 carrot, grated into ribbons

**FOR THE CUCUMBER SALAD**
1 teaspoon Dijon mustard
1 tablespoon balsamic vinegar

3 tablespoons extra virgin olive oil
1 cucumber
Salt and freshly ground black pepper
Sprig of fresh coriander, to garnish

**FOR THE HERB MAYONNAISE**
4 tablespoons mayonnaise
1 tablespoon chopped fresh dill
1 tablespoon chopped fresh mint

For the salad, whisk together the mustard, seasoning, vinegar and oil.
Peel strips off the length of the cucumber, so you are left with stripes of
green. Slice the cucumber and arrange the slices in a bowl. Pour a
little of the vinaigrette over the top. Garnish with the fresh coriander.

Put the mayonnaise in a ramekin and stir in the dill and mint.

Rinse the salmon steaks, pat them dry and brush lightly with oil. Heat
in a heavy-based pan, add the steaks and sear for a minute each side.
Turn the heat down and cook the salmon gently for 6 minutes, or until
the flesh comes away cleanly from the bone.

Meanwhile, gently cook the potatoes in simmering, lightly salted
water for 10–12 minutes, or until just cooked. Blanch the leek strips
and carrot ribbons in boiling water until just tender. Drain all the
vegetables. Put the salmon steaks on warmed plates and arrange
vegetables around them. Serve with the salad and herb mayonnaise.

## P A T R I C K   A N T H O N Y

# RACHEL'S THAILAND TREAT

### Prawns in a creamy Thai-curry sauce, with rice

Rachel Gill and her family love exotic dishes, so she produced prawns and creamed coconut and challenged Patrick to make an oriental treat.

| | |
|---|---|
| **SERVES 4** | A bunch of spring onions |
| Salt | 1 onion, finely chopped |
| 225 g (8 oz) long-grain, Thai jasmine or | 150 ml (5 fl oz) chicken or vegetable stock |
| basmati rice, to serve | Juice and grated zest of 1 lime |
| $\frac{1}{2}$ teaspoon ground turmeric | 100 g (4 oz) button mushrooms, finely sliced |
| | 75 g (3 oz) creamed coconut, grated |
| **FOR THE SAUCE** | $\frac{1}{2}$ teaspoon dried lemon grass |
| Groundnut oil, for frying | $\frac{1}{2}$ teaspoon Thai red or green curry paste |
| 200 g (7 oz) baby corn, halved | 225 g (8 oz) cooked, peeled prawns |
| 200 g (7 oz) mangetout | 150 ml (5 fl oz) double cream |
| $\frac{1}{2}$ fresh green chilli, seeded and | 2 tablespoons chopped fresh coriander, |
| cut in thin strips | to garnish |
| 2.5 cm (1 in) piece of root ginger, | |
| peeled and grated | |

For the rice, pour $\frac{1}{2}$ teaspoon of salt into a large pan of boiling water, add the rice and turmeric and boil for 12 minutes. Drain the rice, put it in a sieve over boiling water, cover it with a tea towel and leave it for 2 minutes, to fluff up.

For the sauce, heat a tablespoon of oil in a frying-pan and, when very hot, add the corn and mangetout and stir-fry them quickly until they are charred on the outside. Then add the chilli, ginger, spring onions, onion, stock, lime juice, mushrooms, creamed coconut, lemon grass and curry paste and cook for 5 minutes over a moderate heat, stirring occasionally. Next add the prawns and cook for just under

2 minutes, to heat them through. Lastly, stir in the cream and heat through for 1–2 minutes. To serve, pour the prawns and sauce on top of a bed of rice and garnish with fresh coriander and zest of lime.

### PATRICK ANTHONY

# JANE'S FRANCO-ORIENTAL PLAICE

Poached plaice with vegetables and creamy mushroom sauce

This recipe combines plaice fillets cooked in a French style – poached in a flavourful court-bouillon and served with a creamy mushroom sauce – with wok-sweet stir-fried vegetables for a refreshingly different oriental-style accompaniment. Jane Atkey, from Surrey, loves entertaining but had never cooked a flat fish like plaice before, so she asked Patrick to show her how.

**SERVES 4**

**FOR THE FISH**
150 ml (5 fl oz) white wine
1 tablespoon lemon juice
4 plaice fillets, skinned
Salt and freshly ground white or black pepper

**FOR THE VEGETABLES**
2 tablespoons sunflower oil
3 leeks, cut into 5 mm (¼ in) slices
225 g (8 oz) carrots, peeled and cut in batons

1 teaspoon soy sauce
100 g (4 oz) spinach, thoroughly washed
100 g (4 oz) mangetout
15 g (½ oz) butter

**FOR THE SAUCE**
35 g (1½ oz) butter
¼ onion, finely chopped
150 ml (5 fl oz) double cream
4 button mushrooms, thinly sliced
Sprigs of fresh parsley, to garnish

For the fish, heat the wine and lemon juice in a large saucepan and season with salt and pepper. Poach the plaice in this court-bouillon (stock) by first bringing the stock to boil; after 30 seconds, remove the pan from the heat, cover and leave it to stand for 3 minutes. Remove the plaice and keep it warm. Strain the bouillon and set it aside.

Heat the oil in a wok and stir-fry the leeks and carrots. When the vegetables are beginning to brown, add the soy sauce.

Put the spinach in a saucepan and cover it with a lid. Put the pan on the heat and cook the spinach in just the water clinging to the leaves for about 40 seconds, or until the leaves have begun to wilt. Drain thoroughly and keep warm.

Blanch the mangetout in a little water for about a minute. Refresh them under cold, running water. Slice them into shreds and fry them quickly in 15 g (1/2 oz) butter, just before serving.

For the sauce, melt the butter in a saucepan, add the onion and cook until softened. Add the reserved fish stock, the double cream, and the mushrooms and cook for 3–4 minutes, until the sauce has reduced a little.

To serve, pile a bed of spinach in the centre of a plate, lay the plaice on top, surround it with the vegetables and pour the sauce over the top. Garnish with fresh parsley sprigs.

---

### READY STEADY COOK Tips

• *Don't be tempted to cook the fillets of plaice for any longer: the texture will not be so good and the fillets may begin to fall apart.*

• *If you have the plaice filleted and skinned for you, ask for the bones. Chop them roughly and add them to the court-bouillon for extra flavour. They will be strained out when the fish has cooked.*

## PATRICK ANTHONY

# SUZY'S TROUT SENSATION

### Pan-fried trout with a rocket butter sauce

Trout is the favourite fish of the husband of Suzy Anthony, from Southgate, London. Suzy wanted a new way to cook trout and also ideas for cooking with rocket, which she had used in salads but not hot.

**SERVES 2**

**FOR THE TROUT**
2 trout
2 tablespoons finely chopped onion
1 tablespoon chopped fresh dill
1 tablespoon chopped fresh tarragon
1 tablespoon chopped fresh parsley
1 teaspoon paprika
1 tablespoon sunflower oil

**FOR THE VEGETABLES**
1 tablespoon sunflower oil

3 carrots, grated
1 large courgette, grated
1 tablespoon soy sauce
2 drops of Tabasco sauce
Salt and freshly ground white or black pepper

**FOR THE SAUCE**
1 egg yolk
1 teaspoon Dijon mustard
2 teaspoons red wine vinegar
40 g (1½ oz) butter, melted
A few rocket leaves, shredded
A few parsley sprigs, to garnish (optional)

Stuff the trout with onion, dill, tarragon and parsley. Season both sides of the trout with the paprika. Pan-fry the fish in a tablespoon of sunflower oil for 8–10 minutes, turning them half-way through.

Fry the carrots and courgette in the remaining tablespoon of oil in a pre-heated wok. Add the soy sauce and Tabasco, season and cook for 3–5 minutes.

Mix the egg yolk, mustard, vinegar and salt and pepper together in a bowl. Whisk in the melted butter; then add the rocket leaves.

To serve, put the trout in the centre of a plate. Spoon courgettes and carrots around the fish and pour over the rocket sauce. Garnish with sprigs of parsley, if you like.

## PATRICK ANTHONY

# DOT'S DELIGHT

### Cod steak with fried potatoes and tomato toasts

Like many people, Dot Kirby, from Harleston, Norfolk, doesn't cook fish. She asked Patrick to create a delicious fish dish that was easy to do and tasty enough to tempt her into becoming a fish-eater.

**SERVES 1**

5 tablespoons sunflower oil
225 g (8 oz) potatoes, peeled and cut in 2 cm (¾ in) cubes
2 garlic cloves, halved
1 sprig of rosemary
50 g (2 oz) piece of smoked streaky bacon, cubed
50 g (2 oz) button mushrooms, sliced

½ teaspoon ginger purée
½ teaspoon balsamic vinegar
175 g (6 oz) thick cod steak
7.5 cm (3 in) French bread, halved lengthways
2 tomatoes, sliced
¼ teaspoon dried oregano
¼ teaspoon dried mixed herbs
Salt and freshly ground pepper
Sprigs of flatleaf parsley, to garnish

Heat 2 tablespoons of oil in a small frying-pan, add the potatoes and fry for 5 minutes. Add the garlic and rosemary to the potatoes and fry for a further 3 minutes, until the potatoes are tender and golden. Remove the garlic and rosemary.

Meanwhile, cook the bacon in a tablespoon of oil for 2 minutes; then add the mushrooms, ginger purée and vinegar and cook gently for 5 minutes, turning occasionally. Heat a tablespoon of oil in a small frying-pan and fry the cod for 5–6 minutes, turning it once.

Toast the slices of bread, cut-side up, until golden. Heat the remaining oil in a small frying-pan, add the tomatoes and sprinkle over the oregano, mixed herbs and seasoning. Cook over a high heat for 2–3 minutes.

Make a bed of potatoes in the centre of a warmed plate. Put the cod steak on top and a piece of bread on each side; arrange the tomatoes on them. Spoon the bacon mixture on top and garnish.

## PATRICK ANTHONY

# GARRY'S PANTOMIME PILLOWS

Puff-pastry pillows of smoked haddock, prawns and mushrooms

In memory of the time stage manager Garry Thomas, from Manchester, played the back end of a pantomime cow, Patrick christened these 'pillows' of puff pastry, filled with a delicious mixture of smoked haddock, prawns and mushrooms in a creamy sauce.

| **SERVES 2** | **FOR THE CABBAGE** |
|---|---|
| Ready-rolled puff pastry, cut in 2 x 10 cm (4 in) squares | 25 g (1 oz) butter |
| 225 g (8 oz) smoked haddock fillet, skinned | 1 tablespoon soft brown sugar |
| 450 ml (15 fl oz) chicken stock | 1 tablespoon soy sauce |
| 150 ml (5 fl oz) white wine | 4–5 drops of Tabasco sauce |
| 2 spring onions | 2–3 tablespoons water |
| 4 tablespoons double cream | ½ green cabbage, shredded |
| 75 g (3 oz) button mushrooms, chopped | Sprigs of parsley, to garnish |
| 75 g (3 oz) peeled prawns | |

Pre-heat the oven to gas mark 7, 220°C (425°F). Line two 10 cm (4 in) tart tins with the pastry and trim the edges (or use a well-greased baking tray). Prick the pastry bases, and bake them for 10–12 minutes. When risen and golden, turn out from the tins and cool.

Poach the fish in the stock for 7–10 minutes. When cooked, discard the stock and flake the haddock in a bowl. Keep warm.

In a frying-pan, bring the white wine to the boil. Add the spring onions and cook for a couple of minutes. Stir in the cream and mushrooms and continue to cook until the sauce reduces and thickens. Add the prawns.

Melt the butter and brown sugar in a frying-pan. Add the soy sauce, Tabasco and water. Stir in the cabbage and cook for 4–5 minutes.

Slice the puff pastry horizontally through the middle, to make a top and bottom.

To serve, place the bases of the puff pastry tarts on a plate. Divide the haddock between each base and spoon over the prawn and mushroom sauce. Then place the lid of the pastry on top. Spoon the cabbage on the side and garnish with fresh parsley.

P A T R I C K   A N T H O N Y

# HEATHER'S HAPPY CRAB

### Dressed crab with home-made mayonnaise

Heather Elliott, from Chesterfield, Derbyshire, used to be a competitive body-builder but is now at home with a young baby. She loves seafood and asked Patrick to show her how to dress a crab. It's well worth making home-made mayonnaise to serve with a fresh crab — simple but delicious.

**SERVES 4**

2 slices of white bread, crusts removed
1 cooked crab, shell-on, weighing 700 g (1½ lb)
3 teaspoons white wine vinegar
2 eggs
1 egg yolk
1 teaspoon Dijon mustard

65 ml (2½ fl oz) sunflower oil
65 ml (2½ fl oz) olive oil
Salt and freshly ground black pepper
½ lettuce, shredded, to serve

**TO GARNISH**
Parsley sprigs
1 lemon, quartered

Make the bread into breadcrumbs.

To dress the crab, twist off the claws and legs. Press down on the mouth end of the crab to split the body apart. Remove and discard the 'dead man's fingers' (part of the stomach, located under the shell). Spoon the brown flesh into a bowl, add salt and pepper, a teaspoon of vinegar and the breadcrumbs. Wash the crab shell, pat it dry, and reserve it.

Crack open the claws and legs with a rolling pin and remove the white flesh. Put it in a separate bowl and set it to one side.

Hard-boil the eggs, piercing a pinhole in the wide end to stop the shell from cracking. When cooked, shell and chop the eggs.

To make the mayonnaise, whisk together the egg yolk, mustard and the remaining 2 teaspoons of vinegar. Add the oil very slowly, whisking vigorously and continuously, until thick. Spoon a little of the mayonnaise over the white crab meat and mash together.

To serve, put the brown flesh into the crab shell and spoon the white meat on top of the brown. On a plate, make a bed of lettuce and arrange the dressed crab on top. Garnish with the chopped egg, parsley and lemon. Serve the rest of the mayonnaise separately.

---

### READY STEADY COOK Tips

• *To stop the mayonnaise from separating, add the oil a drop at a time to start with. When you've added about half the oil, you can pour it in in a slow, steady stream.*

• *If the worst happens and the mayonnaise curdles, don't despair! Start again with a fresh egg yolk and whisk the curdled mixture into it a drop at a time.*

---

Above: Rachel's Delectable Thai Dream (page 10).
Below: Pork and Cider with Ros (page 71).

Above: Garry's Pantomime Pillows (page 30).
Below: Claire's Turkish Creation (page 75).

Above: Ruth's Hoki-coki (page 36).
Below: Sandra's Chilli Sensation (page 59).

Above: Easter Strawberry Nests (page 88).
Below: Terry's Orient Express (page 44).

Above: Mandy's Salmon Marvel (page 24).
Below: Rachel's Ravishing Mushroom Tart (page 14).

Above: Geraldine's Eastern Promise (page 46).
Below: Steak Mother Abbess (page 64).

Above: Dot's Delight (page 29).
Below: Vicky's Pineapple Victory (page 84).

Above: Sarah's Steak Sensation (page 76).
Below: Couscous with Spatchcocked Quail (page 51).

## R I C H A R D   C A W L E Y

# YULE DROOL BREAKFAST

### Kedgeree, savoury croissants and scrambled eggs

This is a triple-decker breakfast spread of kedgeree, ham and cheese croissants and herby scrambled eggs. Jacqueline Walker was expecting her in-laws to join her and her family for Christmas in Fife, Scotland, and she wanted to impress them with a really special Boxing Day breakfast.

**SERVES 2**

**FOR THE KEDGEREE**
50 g (2 oz) white rice, rinsed thoroughly
1 small kipper fillet, skinned
1 small smoked haddock fillet, skinned
15 g (½ oz) butter
¼ onion, chopped
½ teaspoon, garam masala
1 hard-boiled egg, chopped roughly

**FOR THE CROISSANTS**
2 croissants
2 slices of ham
50 g (2 oz) Edam cheese, grated

**FOR THE HERBY SCRAMBLED EGGS**
4 eggs
2 tablespoons double cream
25 g (1 oz) butter
2 tablespoons chopped fresh dill
1 tablespoon chopped fresh parsley
Salt and freshly ground black pepper

Pre-heat the oven to gas mark 6, 200°C (400°F). Bring a pan of water to the boil and cook the rice for about 8–10 minutes. Drain the rice, return it to the pan and set it to one side.

Put the kipper and haddock fillets on some lightly buttered foil and loosely wrap them up. Put the parcel on a baking tray in the oven for 7–8 minutes. Remove and flake the fish.

Meanwhile, melt 15 g (½ oz) of butter in a saucepan, add the onion and cook until soft. Stir in the garam masala. Add the flaked fish, hard-boiled egg and rice and mix well but gently.

Slice open the croissants, and fill them with ham and cheese. Put the croissants in an ovenproof dish and bake for about 6–8 minutes.

To make the herby scrambled eggs, break the eggs into a bowl and whisk lightly together with the cream. Melt the butter in a saucepan, add the egg mixture, the dill and parsley, season and stir continuously over a low heat until scrambled.

To serve, spoon some of the scrambled egg and kedgeree (heat through before serving) on to each plate and accompany with the filled croissants.

## RICHARD CAWLEY

# LITTLE FISHES IN A BASKET

### Pancake baskets with seafood sauce

Scots-born Sylvia Gray, from Tyne and Wear, loves all kinds of fish – especially from the River Tyne, which runs through her home town. Richard served them in pancake baskets, in honour of Shrove Tuesday, when the programme was broadcast.

**SERVES 4**

**FOR THE PANCAKES**
150g (6 oz) plain flour, sifted
3 eggs
450 ml (15 fl oz) milk
Sunflower oil for frying
Salt and freshly ground black pepper

**FOR THE FILLING**
2 red onions, thinly sliced
2 garlic cloves, crushed
400 g (14 oz) tin of tomatoes
1 tablespoon chopped fresh parsley
150 g (6 oz) packet of mixed seafood
150 g (6 oz) packet of crabsticks, chopped
3 tablespoons red wine vinegar
5 tablespoons caster sugar
1 large handful of spinach, thoroughly washed

Pre-heat the oven to gas mark 6, 200°C (400°F). Grease the outside of four ramekins and put them, upside-down, on a baking sheet.

To make the pancake batter, blend the flour, eggs and pinch of salt to a smooth batter. Slowly add the milk and continue to blend until thoroughly mixed.

Heat a little oil in a frying-pan. When it is very hot, pour in a little of the batter, tilting the pan to ensure that the whole base is covered; the pancake should be fairly thick. Make four pancakes of this size. Put a pancake over each upturned ramekin and bake on the middle shelf for 12–14 minutes, or until crisp. Allow the pancakes to cool, then remove the ramekins and turn the pancake baskets over.

Make six more, slightly thinner, pancakes. Stack and slice them so that they resemble tagliatelle. These can be served later as a dessert with lemon and sugar.

For the sauce, fry half a red onion in a tablespoon of oil until soft, covered. Add the garlic and tomatoes and simmer for 5 minutes. Stir in the parsley and continue to simmer. After 5 minutes, add the seafood and crabsticks. Season and cook for a further 2 minutes.

To make the sweet pickled onions, heat the vinegar and sugar together. When the sugar has dissolved, remove from the heat and pour over the remaining onions. Leave for 3–4 minutes; then drain.

To serve, place the spinach leaves around the outside of a large plate. Sprinkle the pickled onions over the spinach. Place the pancake baskets in the centre and fill them with the seafood sauce.

---

### READY STEADY COOK Tips

• *If you don't have the seafood and crabsticks, use prawns and or cubes of white fish, or even flaked canned tuna.*

• *For a vegetarian version, replace the seafood with cubes of tofu or perhaps a fairly firm-textured vegetable such as aubergine.*

## RICHARD CAWLEY

# RUTH'S HOKI-COKI

### Baked fish with carrot and orange salad

Ruth Nelhams, from Kidderminster, loves fishing and it was during her hours spent on the riverbank that she met her future husband. Richard Cawley showed her how to cook New Zealand hoki, a delicious inexpensive white fish, similar to cod in taste and texture, in a paper parcel: 'en papillote'.

**SERVES 2**
1 green pepper, halved and seeded
1 tablespoon olive oil
¼ onion, finely chopped
1 large hoki fillet, halved, or 2 small fillets
1 tomato, chopped
1 tablespoon chopped fresh parsley
Juice of ½ lemon

2 tablespoons double cream
Salt and freshly ground black pepper

**FOR THE SALAD**
4 carrots, peeled and grated
1 orange, peeled and segmented
1 teaspoon balsamic vinegar
Juice of ½ lemon
4 tablespoons olive oil

Pre-heat the oven to gas mark 6, 200°C (400°F). Chop half the pepper finely and cut the rest in thin strips.

Fry the onion and the chopped pepper in the oil. Season and cook for 8 minutes.

Take a large sheet of greaseproof paper and fold it in half. Cut out two large ovals. On to each piece of paper put a piece of hoki fillet. Spoon 2–3 tablespoons of the pepper and onion mixture and a tablespoon of tomatoes on top of each fish. Season with salt and pepper, and add a sprinkle of parsley, a squeeze of lemon juice and a tablespoon of double cream. Seal the papillote by folding over the edge of the paper, leaving a pocket of air over the fish. Put the fish parcels in an ovenproof dish and bake in the preheated oven for about 10 minutes.

For the salad, mix the carrots and orange segments in a bowl. Whisk together the vinegar, lemon juice and oil. Season to taste. Pour the vinaigrette over the carrot and orange salad and spoon the salad on to a plate. Decorate with strips of green pepper. Put a papillote on each plate and serve immediately; each diner opens his or her own parcel at the table, releasing the delicious cooking aroma.

---

### READY STEADY COOK Tips

• *Cooking 'en papillote' is a really good, healthy way to cook all kinds of fish fillets, such as salmon steaks or cutlets. It also works for boneless, skinless chicken breasts and turkey steaks. Vary the aromatics that you add, according to the main ingredient, for example, a little lemon juice, white wine, garlic and chopped fresh herbs for chicken. Adjust the cooking times accordingly.*

• *If your courage fails you and you want to make sure that the fish is cooked before you serve it, just open the parcels and dish them up in the kitchen.*

## RICHARD CAWLEY

# RISING-STAR FISH WITH VEGETABLES

Jennie Eriksen, from Broxbourne, Hertfordshire, brought along some of her Norwegian husband's favourite ingredients and begged for some new ideas for transforming them into a meal to satisfy her six-foot-four husband's huge appetite.

**SERVES 2**

½ aubergine, cut in 5 mm (¼ in) slices
1 tablespoon olive oil

**FOR THE VEGETABLES**
3 tablespoons olive oil
225 g (8 oz) potatoes, cut in 1 cm (½ in) cubes
2 garlic cloves, crushed
1 onion, chopped
1 courgette, cubed
2 tomatoes, chopped

1 teaspoon dried mixed herbs
100 ml (4 fl oz) white wine
1 tablespoon chopped fresh parsley
2 teaspoons tomato purée
Salt and freshly ground black pepper

**FOR THE FISH**
50 g (2 oz) butter
350 g (12 oz) huss (dogfish)
2 tablespoons plain flour, seasoned
Sprigs of flatleaf parsley, to garnish

Pre-heat the oven to gas mark 5, 190°C (375°F). Put the aubergine slices on a lightly oiled baking sheet and brush them very lightly with oil. Roast in the oven for 15 minutes.

Meanwhile, heat 2 tablespoons of oil in a frying-pan, add the potatoes and seasoning and cook for 5 minutes, turning occasionally. Stir in a crushed garlic clove and cook for a further 3–4 minutes, until the potatoes are tender and golden.

Heat the last tablespoon of oil in a frying-pan, add the onion and cook for 3 minutes. Stir in the courgette and the other crushed garlic clove and cook for 3 minutes. Add the tomatoes, mixed herbs, wine, parsley, tomato purée and seasoning and cook for 5 minutes.

# FISH DISHES

Clarify the butter by melting it in a small pan over a gentle heat, spooning off any white foam which comes to the surface. Then carefully pour off the clear golden liquid, leaving any sediment at the bottom of the pan. Cut the fish into two equal pieces and remove the backbone by cutting either side with a sharp knife, but not cutting right through. Carefully cut out the bone and lie the flesh flat. Coat the pieces in the seasoned flour and shake off the excess. Heat 2 tablespoons of clarified butter in a frying-pan, add the fish and cook it for 6–8 minutes, turning once, until lightly browned.

To serve, put four slices of roasted aubergine on each serving plate. Place the fish on top and spoon the potatoes and courgette mixture around the edge. Garnish with a sprig of flatleaf parsley.

---

### READY STEADY COOK Tips

• *Clarifying the butter is really worthwhile, because it allows you to heat the butter high enough for a good frying temperature, without the risk of the milky residue burning. Clarified butter keeps well in the refrigerator.*

• *Roasting vegetables in the oven gives them a wonderfully sweet flavour and a delicious skin. Branch out from the usual potatoes and parsnips: try aubergines, as here, cloves of garlic, halved peppers, tomatoes, leeks, celery, courgettes and other squashes. The choice is almost limitless and it's such an easy, no-fuss way of serving a wider than usual variety of vegetables.*

# POULTRY AND GAME

## RICHARD CAWLEY

# TURKEY ESCALOPES WITH BEURRE BLANC SAUCE

*Married, with seven children and another on the way, Janet Meredith from Manchester was hoping for a new idea for serving ever-popular poultry. This marinated turkey recipe has lots of flavour and is ready in next to no time.*

| SERVES 4 | FOR THE BEURRE BLANC SAUCE |
|---|---|
| 150 ml (5 fl oz) white wine | 300 ml (10 fl oz) chicken stock |
| 3 tablespoons soy sauce | 2 tablespoons white wine |
| 1 tablespoon cornflour, blended with | 2.5 cm (1 in) root ginger, peeled and chopped |
| a little cold water | 2 spring onions, roughly chopped |
| 4 turkey escalopes | 1 tablespoon soy sauce |
| 1 broccoli, cut in florets | 75 g (3 oz) butter, cubed |
| 1 cauliflower, cut in florets | Chopped fresh parsley and coriander, |
| ½ head of Chinese leaves, sliced | to garnish |
| Olive oil, for shallow-frying | |

To make the marinade, mix the white wine, soy sauce and cornflour. Add the turkey and chill for up to an hour.

Steam the broccoli and cauliflower in 1 cm of hot salted water in a large covered pan for 4–5 minutes, shaking the pan occasionally. Add the Chinese leaves and cook for 2 minutes more.

Remove the escalopes from the marinade and let them drain briefly. Pat them dry. Heat the oil in a frying-pan and fry the escalopes for 5–6 minutes on each side. Discard the marinade. You can cut the meat into strips to reduce the cooking time to 4–5 minutes.

For the sauce, put all the ingredients, except the butter, in a pan and reduce by two-thirds. Strain out the ginger and spring onions. Whisk in the cubes of cold butter over a low heat; do not allow to boil. Put the escalopes on warmed plates, pour over the sauce and garnish with chopped parsley and coriander.

## RICHARD CAWLEY

# DEBBIE'S LEMON CHICKEN

This is a delicious Chinese-style dish with a lemony sauce, easily made without resorting to jars of ready-made Chinese sauces. Debbie Courtney, from Epsom, Surrey, is a busy mum and self-confessed hopeless cook who relies on packet mixes and jars. She wanted Richard to show her a tasty meal prepared from fresh ingredients.

**SERVES 2**

**FOR THE CHICKEN**
75 g (3 oz) plain flour
½ teaspoon bicarbonate of soda
150 ml (5 fl oz) water
1 tablespoon white wine vinegar
Sunflower oil, for deep-frying
4 boneless, skinless chicken thighs, cut in small pieces

**FOR THE SAUCE**
3–4 shallots, chopped
1 tablespoon olive oil
150 ml (5 fl oz) white wine
1 heaped teaspoon cornflour
Juice of 1 lemon
1 teaspoon honey

**FOR THE POTATO SALAD**
450 g (1 lb) potatoes, scrubbed and cut in chunks
2 tablespoons olive oil
A squeeze of lemon juice
½ tablespoon white wine vinegar

**FOR THE COLESLAW**
1 tablespoon Greek yoghurt
1 tablespoon mayonnaise
½ teaspoon Dijon mustard
100 g (4 oz) coleslaw mix
1 green pepper, seeded and thinly sliced
Salt and freshly ground black pepper

**TO GARNISH**
Lemon wedges
1 tomato, quartered

For the deep-fried chicken, make a batter by mixing together the flour, bicarbonate of soda, water and the wine vinegar. Heat the oil until it's very hot. Dip the chicken pieces in the batter and deep-fry them for 4 minutes, until golden brown. Drain on absorbent kitchen paper.

To make the lemon sauce, sauté the shallots in the oil for 2 minutes. Add the wine and simmer for 3 minutes. Meanwhile, mix together the cornflour, lemon juice and a little water, to form a runny paste. Add this to the shallots, bring to the boil and allow the sauce to thicken. Stir in the honey and cook for a further minute.

For the potato salad, boil the potato cubes in water for 12–15 minutes. Drain the potatoes and pour over the olive oil, lemon juice and vinegar. Season and toss the potatoes.

To make the coleslaw dressing, mix together the yoghurt, mayonnaise, mustard and salt and pepper. Pour over the coleslaw and green pepper and mix thoroughly.

To serve, arrange the chicken pieces on a plate, accompanied by the lemon sauce and the warm potato salad. Garnish with lemon wedges and tomato quarters. Serve the coleslaw separately.

---

### READY STEADY COOK Tips

• *For a simpler, yet delicious, supper, still with the Chinese theme, just serve the chicken with the lemon sauce and some plain boiled rice.*

• *Turkey steaks or boneless, tender pork, cut in strips, could be treated in the same way and would go very well with the lemon and honey sauce. Vegetarians could try cubes of tofu.*

## RICHARD CAWLEY

# TERRY'S ORIENT EXPRESS

Chicken in ginger and pineapple sauce, with pineapple slices and ginger pancakes

**Richard thought up this idea for a home-made oriental banquet for the ingredients brought along by Terry Gould, a lover of Chinese food, from Nottingham.**

**SERVES 2**

4 chicken thighs
3 tablespoons soy sauce
Sunflower oil, for frying
150 ml (5 fl oz) white wine

**FOR THE SAUCE**
½ onion, finely chopped
½ green pepper, seeded and finely chopped
1 celery stick, chopped
1 teaspoon root ginger, grated
1 garlic clove, crushed

200 g (7 oz) tin of pineapple in natural juice
Juice of 1 lime
75 ml (3 fl oz) white wine

**FOR THE PANCAKES**
100 g (4 oz) plain flour
1 heaped teaspoon baking powder
½ teaspoon grated root ginger
1 egg, beaten
135 ml (4½ fl oz) milk
Salt and freshly ground black pepper

Marinate the chicken in the soy sauce, ideally for at least 30 minutes. Remove the chicken, reserving the marinade, and pat it dry.

Heat 2 tablespoons of oil in a frying-pan. Fry the chicken skin-side down first. Once the skin is brown, cook the other side for a couple of minutes. Add the wine. Bring to the boil, cover and simmer for 10–12 minutes, until the chicken is cooked.

Meanwhile, in a different pan, heat another 2 tablespoons of oil and sauté the chopped onion, pepper and celery. Add the ginger, garlic, pineapple juice, lime juice and white wine. Season and simmer for 10 minutes.

Fry the pineapple slices in hot oil until golden brown.

For the pancakes, put the flour, baking powder, a pinch of salt and the reserved soy sauce in a bowl. Mix well and then add the ginger and beaten egg. Mix thoroughly whilst adding the milk and continue to beat until the mixture has a thick consistency.

Heat another 2 tablespoons of oil in a frying-pan and, when very hot, tip 3 tablespoons of the batter for each pancake into the pan, tilt the pan to spread the batter out to 10–12 cm (4–5 inches), and fry until lightly browned each side. The pancakes should be thick and puffy. Make another three pancakes in this way.

To serve, put the chicken on a plate and spoon the sauce over it. Place the ginger pancakes on the side and put a pineapple slice on top of each pancake.

---

### READY STEADY COOK Tips

• *Marinating in soy sauce is an easy way to add delicious savoury flavours to relatively mild-flavoured meat, such as chicken, turkey or pork. You could make a vegetarian version of this dish using tofu.*

• *The ginger pancakes would be good as a dessert topped with a good syrupy sauce or fruit. As with this recipe, you can use pineapple or you can accompany them with poached pears, which go very well with ginger.*

---

## RICHARD CAWLEY

# GERALDINE'S EASTERN PROMISE

### Thai chicken curry, with lemon rice and sesame beans

Geraldine Corbett, from Haslington, near Crewe, loves curries and oriental spices, but isn't very confident about cooking with them. She brought in some chicken and typical Thai flavourings and asked Richard to show her how to make a Thai-style curry from them.

**SERVES 2**

**FOR THE RICE**
175 g (6 oz) Thai fragrant rice
½ teaspoon ground turmeric
Grated zest of 2 lemons and juice of ½ a lemon

**FOR THE CHICKEN**
1 tablespoon sunflower oil
1 small onion, chopped
350 g (12 oz) boneless, skinless chicken thighs cut in 2.5 cm (1 in) chunks
2 garlic cloves, finely chopped

2.5 cm (1 in) piece root ginger, finely chopped
1 teaspoon lemon-grass paste
Tabasco sauce
200 ml (7 fl oz) coconut milk

**FOR THE BEANS**
1 tablespoon sesame seeds
1 teaspoon demerara sugar
1 tablespoon soy sauce
Juice of ½ a lime
Tabasco sauce
225 g (8 oz) green beans, cut in 5 cm (2 in) lengths
Sprigs of fresh coriander, to garnish

Cook the rice in a pan of boiling water, with the turmeric and lemon zest and juice for 8–10 minutes, until tender.

Meanwhile, heat the oil, add the onion and cook for a minute. Add the chicken, garlic and ginger and cook for 2 minutes. Stir in the lemon-grass paste and a few drops of Tabasco sauce and cook for 2 minutes. Add the coconut milk and simmer for 8–10 minutes, stirring now and again.

Dry-fry the sesame seeds in a small frying-pan for 3 minutes, until golden. In a pestle and mortar, grind them to a coarse paste. Add the sugar, soy sauce, lime juice and a few drops of Tabasco sauce and mix well.

Cook the beans in a pan of boiling water for 3 minutes. Drain well and toss in the sesame dressing.

To serve, spoon the rice, coconut chicken and sesame beans on to serving plates and garnish with fresh coriander.

---

### READY STEADY COOK Tips

• *If you can't find Thai fragrant rice, substitute basmati rice.*

• *If you have a nearby Oriental food shop and can buy fresh lime leaves, adding a couple of them to the coconut sauce will enhance the fragrant lemony flavour of the lemon-grass, for a really authentic Thai flavour.*

• *Leftover coconut milk can be added to other curries and stir-fries to make them deliciously creamy and add a subtle coconut flavour to the blend of spices. Or use it instead of cream with sliced tropical fruit or for unusual and exotic milkshakes.*

---

## RICHARD CAWLEY

# EMMA AND ANNA'S CHICKEN AND PASTA DINNER

### Breadcrumbed chicken with creamy pasta sauce

The family of Kirstin Whybrow, from Hatfield, Hertfordshire, love pasta, chicken and anything with a sauce. She wanted Richard to show her how to make a pasta sauce without any lumps, using spinach. Richard came up with this idea for breadcrumbed chicken, served with carrots and leeks and accompanied by pasta with a creamy leek and spinach sauce.

| | |
|---|---|
| **SERVES 2** | 2 carrots, cut in fine matchsticks |
| 175 g (6 oz) fusilli, bucati lunghi or spaghetti | 2 leeks, cut in fine matchsticks |
| 225 g (8 oz) boneless, skinless chicken breast | 1 garlic clove, crushed |
| 2 tablespoons plain flour, seasoned | 150 ml (5 fl oz) double cream |
| 1 egg, beaten | 225 g (8 oz) spinach, washed and trimmed |
| 50 g (2 oz) breadcrumbs | Juice of 1/2 an orange |
| 3 tablespoons olive oil | Salt and freshly ground black pepper |
| 45 g (1¾ oz) butter | Sprigs of flatleaf parsley, to garnish |

Cook the pasta in a pan of boiling, salted water for 8–10 minutes until just tender. Drain.

Meanwhile, wrap the chicken loosely in cling film and bash it with a rolling pin until it's 5 mm (1/4 in) thick. Cut the chicken in half, if you like. Coat it in the flour, dip it in the egg and coat it with the breadcrumbs. Heat a tablespoon of oil and 15 g (1/2 oz) of the butter in a frying-pan, add the chicken and cook it over a moderate heat for 8 minutes, until cooked through and golden, turning once.

Heat another tablespoon of oil and 15 g (1/2 oz) of butter in a pan, add the carrots and half of the leeks and cook them gently for 8 minutes.

Heat the final tablespoon of oil and 15 g (½ oz) of butter in another pan, add the rest of the leeks and then cook them gently for 2 minutes. Add the garlic and cook for a minute. Stir in the cream and seasoning and leave to simmer for 3 minutes. Add the spinach and cook for another 3 minutes. Stir the orange juice and seasoning into the pan of carrots and leek. Then stir the pasta into the cream and spinach sauce and cook for a minute to reheat the pasta; spoon into a serving bowl.

Divide the chicken in two, if necessary, put the chicken on warmed serving plates, with the carrots and leeks, and garnish with sprigs of flatleaf parsley.

## RICHARD CAWLEY

# TURKEY BALLS WITH RICE

Becky Thould is from Evesham, Worcester, but is a student at Swansea University, where she is studying sociology and anthropology. Like students everywhere, Becky is on a tight budget and she asked Richard to cook her a luxury meal at an affordable price. Richard obliged with this idea for minced turkey in a creamy sauce, served with slightly spiced carrots and leeks, tomato rice and a crisp, refreshing carrot salad.

**SERVES 4**

| | |
|---|---|
| 225 g (8 oz) long-grain rice | 1 egg |
| 400 g (14 oz) tin of chopped tomatoes, drained, juice reserved | 4 tablespoons olive oil |
| 2 garlic cloves | 2 leeks, sliced |
| 1 tablespoon chopped fresh flatleaf parsley | 3 carrots |
| 1 tablespoon chopped fresh basil | A pinch of garam masala |
| 450 g (1 lb) minced turkey | 150 ml (5 fl oz) double cream |
| 100 g (4 oz) fresh breadcrumbs | 1 tablespoon tomato purée |
| | Salt and freshly ground black pepper |

Put the rice in a pan, with the juice from the tomatoes. Top up with water to come 1 cm (½ in) above the rice; then add the tomato flesh, 1 finely chopped garlic clove and seasoning. Simmer for 5 minutes. Then add the parsley and basil and simmer for another 5 minutes, until the rice is tender and the water has been absorbed. Cover to keep warm.

Put the turkey, remaining garlic clove, breadcrumbs, egg and seasoning in a food processor and whizz until thoroughly mixed. Shape the mixture into walnut-sized balls. Heat a tablespoon of oil in a large frying-pan, add the turkey balls and cook them for 13–15 minutes over a moderate heat, turning now and again, until they are cooked through and golden brown.

Heat 2 tablespoons of oil in a pan, add the leeks and cook for 2 minutes. Slice two carrots and add them to the leeks, with the garam masala. Cook for a further 4 minutes, stirring occasionally.

Grate the remaining carrot. Mix 1 tablespoon of oil with plenty of seasoning and pour it over the grated carrot.

Add the cream and tomato purée to the turkey balls and heat through for 1 minute. Pile the rice on a serving plate, top with the turkey balls and cream sauce. Spoon the leeks and carrots around the edge. Serve the grated carrot salad separately.

---

### READY STEADY COOK Tip

• *Minced turkey is economical and delicious and low in saturated fat. Try substituting it for beef mince for a change in a variety of dishes, for example, chilli con carne. You don't have to confine it to dishes with creamy sauces.*

## RICHARD CAWLEY

# COUSCOUS WITH SPATCHCOCKED QUAIL

The family of Tracey Burgess, from Rushden, Northants, all love food and are happy to try anything new. Tracey brought some quail for Richard to cook, which she thought would be an interesting alternative to chicken, and Richard thought up this way of spatchcocking quail with two skewers and serving it with couscous, as a change from rice, and raw and cooked vegetables.

| | |
|---|---|
| **SERVES 2** | 4 celery sticks, 2 chopped, 2 sliced thinly |
| 2 quails | 600 ml (1 pint) chicken stock |
| Juice of 1 lime | 6 tomatoes, cut into small wedges |
| 1 tablespoon soy sauce | 50 g (2 oz) sultanas |
| 1 tablespoon clear honey | 25 g (1 oz) butter |
| 1 tablespoon sesame oil | 175 g (6 oz) couscous |
| Tabasco sauce | A small handful of fresh chives, snipped in |
| 2 garlic cloves, crushed | 2.5 cm (1 in) lengths |
| 2 tablespoons sunflower oil | Salt and freshly ground black pepper |
| 1 onion, chopped | Fresh chives, to garnish |

Using kitchen scissors, cut along both sides of the backbone of each quail and remove the backbone. Open out the quails and flatten them with the heel of your hand. Push two 20 cm (8 in) skewers diagonally through each quail. (If using bamboo skewers, soak them in water for at least 30 minutes, to stop them from burning during cooking.)

Mix the lime juice, soy sauce, honey, sesame oil, a few drops of Tabasco sauce, 1 crushed garlic clove and seasoning. Put the quails on a grill rack and brush over half of the lime-juice mixture. Cook under a moderately hot grill for 12–15 minutes, turning once.

Meanwhile, heat the oil in a pan, add the onion, chopped celery and remaining garlic clove and cook for 3 minutes. Add 150 ml

(5 fl oz) stock, three-quarters of the tomatoes, the sultanas, a few more drops of Tabasco sauce and seasoning. Simmer for 5 minutes.

Melt the butter in a pan, add the couscous, the rest of the stock and seasoning. Bring to the boil and simmer for 3–4 minutes, until the couscous is light and fluffy.

Make a salad with the sliced celery, remaining tomatoes and the snipped chives. Drizzle over the remaining marinade mixture as a dressing and toss everything together. Put the cooked vegetables on a serving plate and add the couscous. Top with the grilled quail and garnish with fresh chives. Serve with the salad.

## RICHARD CAWLEY

# VIV'S HIGHLAND FLING

Venison steak in a white-wine and mustard sauce, on a bed of potato and marrow

Viv Fetherston's family have been on a low-fat diet since her husband's heart attack. She brought along venison as a real treat for him.

**SERVES 2**

2 x 225 g (8 oz) venison steaks
3 tablespoons olive oil
1 onion, finely chopped
75 ml (3 fl oz) white wine
1 teaspoon butter
1 teaspoon Dijon mustard
1 teaspoon honey
1/2 teaspoon Worcestershire sauce
2 teaspoons Greek yoghurt
1 potato, peeled and diced

1/4 marrow, seeded, cut in 5 mm (1/4 in) slices and then in fine strips
2 sprigs of fresh rosemary
1 tablespoon chopped fresh parsley

**FOR THE SALAD**
400g (14 oz) tin of haricot beans, drained
1 garlic clove, finely chopped
1 tablespoon chopped fresh mint
1 tablespoon chopped fresh dill
Juice of 1/2 orange

Cover the venison steak in cling film and flatten it with a rolling pin; then cut it in 5 mm (¼ in) strips. Heat a tablespoon of the olive oil in a frying-pan, add the venison and sear on both sides over a high heat for about 3–4 minutes for each side. Remove and put in a casserole dish and keep warm.

Using the same pan, add half of the onion and fry in the leftover venison juices, pour in the wine and reduce it. Add the butter, Dijon mustard, honey, Worcestershire sauce and cook for 3–4 minutes. Finally, stir in the Greek yoghurt and a little water and reduce for a further 2–3 minutes.

Meanwhile, heat the remaining oil in a wok, add the potato and marrow, half of the remaining onion, the rosemary and parsley and stir-fry until softened.

For the side salad, mix together the haricot beans, remaining onion, garlic, mint, dill and juice of the orange in a bowl. To serve, lay the venison on a bed of potato and marrow and pour the sauce over. Serve the salad separately.

---

### READY STEADY COOK Tips

• *If you can't get venison steak, this would work just as well using fillet steak.*

• *Try another kind of bean in the salad: there are many kinds available in cans for convenience, such as cannellini beans, kidney beans and chick-peas.*

• *Flattening the meat with a rolling pin helps to tenderise it, which is helpful when you are only going to cook it for a brief time.*

---

## PATRICK ANTHONY

# JULIE'S ALPINE JOY

### Cheese-topped chicken with salsify sauce

Julie Ritzman now lives in Lufingen, Switzerland, but she enjoys *Ready Steady Cook* via the World Service. Julie brought along some Swiss cheese and salsify, a vegetable that tastes a little like asparagus, in search of new ways to impress her Swiss husband and three children.

| SERVES 2 | |
| --- | --- |
| 25 g (1 oz) butter | 2 boneless, skinless chicken breasts |
| 25 g (1 oz) plain flour | 1 tablespoon sunflower oil |
| 300 ml (10 fl oz) milk | 100 g (4 oz) Emmenthal cheese, grated |
| 400 g (14 oz) tin of salsify, drained, or | 1 onion, sliced in thin rings |
| asparagus or turnips, blanched until tender | 225 g (8 oz) broccoli, cut into florets |
| crisp and diced | 1 tablespoon chopped fresh parsley (optional) |
| 1 tablespoon chopped fresh dill | Salt and freshly ground black pepper |

Pre-heat the oven to gas mark 6, 200°C (400°F). Whisk together the butter, flour and milk in a pan to make a white sauce. Bring to boil and leave to simmer for 6 minutes, stirring occasionally, to let the flour cook out and the sauce thicken. Add the salsify, or asparagus or turnips, and dill and cook until the salsify has warmed through.

Bash the chicken breasts with a rolling pin, to tenderize them. Season the chicken breasts. Heat the oil and fry the chicken for 5 minutes on each side. Transfer the chicken to a shallow casserole dish and bake for 8–10 minutes. Sprinkle the cheese over the chicken and put it under a hot grill, until the cheese has melted and turned golden brown.

Meanwhile, sauté the onion rings in the pan in which the chicken was fried for 6–8 minutes, until they begin to caramelize. Boil or steam the broccoli florets, until just tender.

To serve, garnish a plate with the broccoli. Arrange the chicken breasts in the centre, with the onions on top, and surround with the salsify in white sauce. Garnish with chopped parsley, if you like.

## RICHARD CAWLEY

# CHICKEN AVE MARIA

Fried chicken with bulghar wheat and tomato and orange salad

Abby Arnold, from Walsall, West Midlands, is a student at Oxford University, a member of a choral group and a keen cook. She brought along chicken, spices and bulghar wheat, in the hope that Richard would create an interesting dish.

**SERVES 2**

| | |
|---|---|
| 2 large chicken thighs | 1 onion |
| 2 tablespoons plain flour | 1 green pepper, seeded |
| 1 teaspoon ground cumin | 1 garlic clove, crushed |
| 1 teaspoon ground cinnamon | ½ fresh green chilli, seeded and chopped |
| A pinch of cayenne pepper | 6 tomatoes, chopped |
| 1 egg, beaten | 3 tablespoons white wine |
| 100 g (4 oz) plus 6 tablespoons bulghar wheat | 25 g (1 oz) sultanas |
| 4 tablespoons olive oil | 1 orange, peeled and sliced |
| 750 ml (1¼ pint) chicken stock | Salt and freshly ground black pepper |
| | Sprigs of coriander, to garnish |

Cut half-way through each chicken thigh and open it out. Mix the flour, ½ teaspoon of cumin, ½ teaspoon of cinnamon, the cayenne pepper and seasoning. Coat the chicken thighs in the seasoned flour and then dip them in the beaten egg. Coat with the 6 tablespoons of bulghar wheat. Heat 2 tablespoons of oil in a frying-pan, add the chicken and cook over a moderate heat for 15 minutes, turning now and again, until cooked through.

Put the stock in a pan and bring it to the boil. Add the 100 g (4 oz) bulghar wheat and simmer for 10 minutes.

Chop half of the onion and three-quarters of the green pepper. Heat a tablespoon of oil in a pan, add the chopped onion and pepper, garlic and chilli and cook for 3 minutes. Stir in the remaining cumin and cinnamon and cook for a minute. Add two-thirds of the chopped tomatoes, the wine, sultanas and seasoning and cook for 5 minutes.

Finely slice the rest of the onion and green pepper. Mix with the remaining chopped tomatoes and put in a salad bowl. Arrange the orange slices around the edge. Season the salad and drizzle over a tablespoon of oil.

Drain the bulghar wheat and pile it in the centre of two serving plates. Put the chicken on top and spoon the vegetable stew around the edge. Garnish with sprigs of coriander. Serve with the salad.

## PATRICK ANTHONY

# WENDY'S CHICKEN-LIVER DOUBLE DELIGHT

Chicken livers are inexpensive, nutritious and delicious. Supermarket checkout-operator Wendy Hunt, from Swindon, had never tasted or cooked with them, so Patrick showed her not just one but two delicious ideas for using them: in a creamy sauce with pasta and in a warm salad with crisp bacon.

**SERVES 2**

**FOR THE PASTA DISH**
6 'nests' or 175 g (6 oz) multicoloured tagliatelle
1 tablespoon olive oil
1 red onion, chopped
1 tablespoon sunflower oil
225 g (8 oz) chicken livers, trimmed, ½ finely chopped, ½ cut in bite-sized pieces
1 garlic clove, finely chopped
2 tablespoons white wine vinegar
120 ml (4 fl oz) double cream

**FOR THE WARM SALAD**
2 rashers smoked back bacon, chopped
1 tablespoon balsamic vinegar
1 tablespoon olive oil
½ small round lettuce
4 radicchio leaves
½ small ripe avocado, peeled and cubed
5 yellow or red cherry tomatoes, quartered
¼ small cucumber, cut in ribbons
Salt and freshly ground black pepper
Sprigs of flatleaf parsley, to garnish

For the pasta dish, cook the pasta according to the instructions on the packet. Drain, toss in the olive oil and keep warm.

Sauté the onion in the sunflower oil for 2 minutes, until the onions become translucent. Add the chopped chicken livers, garlic and white wine vinegar. Stir-fry briskly for 4 minutes, then season and add the cream to heat through and reduce slightly.

Serve the tagliatelle on a platter, with the creamy chicken-liver sauce.

For the warm salad, fry the chicken-liver pieces, bacon and balsamic vinegar in a tablespoon of olive oil. Season and cook for 4–5 minutes.

To serve, tear up the lettuce leaves and arrange them on a platter, with the radicchio leaves, avocado, tomatoes and cucumber. Spoon the livers and bacon in the centre of the salad and garnish with flatleaf parsley sprigs.

---

### READY STEADY COOK Tips

• *Always trim chicken livers, to remove any tubes and any greenish parts, which may have a bitter taste. Be careful not to overcook chicken livers; they should only just cook through or they will be tough and unpalatable.*

• *Warm salads make excellent light meals when you want something quick but don't feel like a plate of completely cold food. They are also good dinner-party starters, as you can make a small amount of an expensive ingredient, such as scallops or duck livers, go a long way.*

---

## PATRICK ANTHONY

# RITA'S REMARKABLE RABBIT

### Rabbit with Stilton sauce and fried potatoes

Rita Burton has always wanted to learn how to cook rabbit. She and her husband, Ted, who live in High Wycombe, Bucks, don't like boring food, so Patrick thought up this delicious bacon and Stilton sauce, which will really bring out the delicate flavour of rabbit, served with crisp, deep-fried potatoes.

**SERVES 2**

- 350 g (12 oz) skinless, boneless rabbit portions
- 3 tablespoons sunflower oil
- ½ teaspoon dried oregano
- 15 g (½ oz) butter
- 1 small onion, finely chopped
- 50 g (2 oz) unsmoked back bacon, cubed
- 4 tablespoons double cream
- 50 g (2 oz) Stilton cheese, crumbled
- 1 tablespoon soy sauce
- Oil for deep-frying
- 350 g (12 oz) potatoes, cut in 2 cm (¾ in) cubes
- 2 carrots
- 1 tablespoon chopped fresh coriander
- Salt and freshly ground black pepper
- Sprigs of flatleaf parsley and chives, to garnish

Put the rabbit portions between two sheets of foil or cling film and beat them with a rolling pin until they are just 5 mm (¼ in) thick. Season with pepper and fry in 2 tablespoons of oil for 8 minutes, until cooked through, turning once half-way. Season with salt and oregano.

Meanwhile, heat the remaining tablespoon of oil and the butter in a frying-pan, add the onion and bacon and cook for 5 minutes. Stir in the cream, Stilton, soy sauce and black pepper and simmer for 2 minutes.

Heat the oil for deep-frying to 190°C (375°F). Deep-fry the potatoes for 3 minutes, until golden and tender. Drain on absorbent kitchen paper. Cut the carrots into ribbons with a vegetable peeler and blanch them in a pan of boiling water for 2 minutes. Drain and season well.

To serve, put the rabbit on a plate and pour over the Stilton sauce. Put the potatoes and carrots around the rabbit, sprinkle coriander over the carrots and garnish with sprigs of parsley and chives.

## PATRICK ANTHONY

# SANDRA'S CHILLI SENSATION

Turkey chilli with tortillas, re-fried beans and yoghurt-chilli dip

A lover of spicy food, Sandra Wisden brought along kidney beans and soft tortillas in the hope that Patrick would create a chilli recipe with a difference. Patrick obliged with this delicious recipe using turkey as an alternative to minced beef and intriguingly flavoured with cocoa powder.

**SERVES 2**

**FOR THE RE-FRIED BEANS**
40 g (1½ oz) butter
400 g (14 oz) tin of red kidney beans, drained
1 teaspoon ground cumin
¼ teaspoon hot chilli powder

**FOR THE CHILLI**
1 tablespoon sunflower oil
15 g (½ oz) butter
2 spring onions, sliced
½ green pepper, seeded and chopped
200 g (7 oz) tin of chopped tomatoes
1 tablespoon tomato purée
225 g (8 oz) turkey-breast stir-fry strips

1 teaspoon ground cumin
¼ teaspoon hot chilli powder
1 teaspoon dried oregano
½ teaspoon cocoa powder
3 tablespoons double cream
2 teaspoons lemon juice
Salt and freshly ground black pepper

**TO SERVE**
4 spring onions
150 g (5 oz) Greek yoghurt
1 tablespoon chopped pickled green jalapeño chillies
6 soft flour tortillas
Sprigs of flatleaf parsley, to garnish

Cut 5 cm (2 in) from the base of the four spring onions from the garnish and, leaving the root end intact, thinly slice each one lengthways. Put the pieces in a bowl of iced water and set them aside, to curl.

Melt 40 g (1½ oz) of butter in a pan, add the kidney beans and mash them with a potato masher until they are almost smooth. Stir in a teaspoon of cumin, ¼ teaspoon of chilli powder and seasoning and cook gently for 10 minutes, stirring frequently.

Meanwhile, heat the oil and 15 g (½ oz) butter in a frying-pan, add the sliced onions and green pepper and cook for 2 minutes. Stir in the chopped tomatoes and tomato purée and then push to one side of the frying-pan. Add the turkey to the other side of the frying-pan and stir in the remaining cumin and chilli, the oregano, cocoa powder and seasoning. Cook for 3 minutes and then stir the turkey and vegetables together and cook for 8–10 minutes.

Mix the yoghurt and jalapeños together and spoon into a serving bowl. Heat the tortillas, one at a time, in a hot, dry frying-pan for 1–2 minutes, turning once.

Stir the cream and lemon juice into the turkey chilli and cook for 1 minute. To serve, fold two of the tortillas in quarters and put them on the side of a serving plate. Fold under the edges of another tortilla and put it in the centre of the plate. Spoon half of the turkey chilli on top of the middle tortilla and spoon two heaps of the re-fried beans next to the quartered tortillas. Repeat with the second serving plate. Garnish with the spring onion curls and sprigs of flatleaf parsley.

---

### READY STEADY COOK Tips

• *You can use soured cream instead of the double cream and lemon juice, if you like.*

• *Chocolate is a traditional flavouring in South American savoury dishes. It doesn't make the dish sweet but adds a rich depth to the savoury flavours.*

PATRICK ANTHONY

# PATRICIA'S SCRUMPY CHRISTMAS

Pasta with chicken and cider sauce, and carrot puffs

On a programme close to Christmas, Patricia Thornborough, from the Isle of Wight, produced some locally made cider, which Patrick used in a delicious sauce for chicken served with pasta. He also made golden, crisp, deep-fried carrot puffs, accompanied by a tangy dip.

**SERVES 2**

**FOR THE CARROT PUFFS**
2 carrots, grated
1 leek, halved lengthways and finely sliced, or
4 spring onions, finely chopped
2 tablespoons plain flour
1 teaspoon baking powder
2 eggs, beaten
¼ teaspoon chilli powder

**FOR THE DIP**
4 tablespoons mayonnaise
2 teaspoons tomato ketchup
½ teaspoon Worcestershire sauce
A few drops of Tabasco sauce

**FOR THE CHICKEN WITH PASTA**
Oil for deep-frying
175 g (6 oz) egg and spinach tagliatelle
2 tablespoons sunflower oil
350 g (12 oz) boneless, skinless chicken breasts, cut in 5 cm (2 in) chunks
150 ml (5 fl oz) scrumpy or dry cider
1 tablespoon wholegrain or garlic mustard
15 g (½ oz) butter
1 leek, halved lengthways and finely sliced
75 g (3 oz) button mushrooms, sliced
75 ml (3 fl oz) double cream
Salt and freshly ground black pepper
Fresh chives, to garnish

Put all the ingredients for the carrot puffs in a bowl and season. Mix well; then set aside. For the dip, mix the mayonnaise, tomato ketchup, Worcestershire sauce, Tabasco sauce and seasoning, to make a dip. Spoon into a serving bowl and set aside.

Heat the oil for deep-frying to 190°C (375°F). Add heaped teaspoonsful of the carrot mixture to the hot oil and deep-fry them for 1–2 minutes, until they are puffed up and golden. Drain on kitchen paper and keep hot while cooking the rest of the carrot puffs.

Cook the tagliatelle in a pan of boiling water for 8–10 minutes. Heat a tablespoon of oil in a frying-pan, add the chicken and cook for 8 minutes, turning occasionally. Add the cider, mustard and seasoning and simmer for 5 minutes.

Melt the butter and remaining tablespoon of oil in a pan, add the rest of the leeks and cook for 3 minutes. Add the mushrooms and cook for 2 minutes. Add the leeks and mushrooms to the chicken, with the cream, and leave to simmer for 2 minutes.

Serve the carrot puffs with the mayonnaise dip, garnished with fresh chives. Serve the scrumpy chicken with the tagliatelle.

---

### READY STEADY COOK Tips

• *Always check that pasta is cooked perfectly by biting a piece: it should be tender but still have a slight bite to it in the centre. The Italians call this 'al dente'.*

• *Cider can be used instead of white wine in a lot of recipes. It goes very well with pork as well as chicken and, of course, with anything with apples.*

---

# MEAT DISHES

## RICHARD CAWLEY

# STEAK MOTHER ABBESS

### Steak with red-wine sauce, mashed potatoes and spinach

Dorothy Bell, from Bradford, is famous locally for her role as Mother Abbess in *The Sound of Music*, so Richard christened this recipe for her favourite food, fillet steak, in her honour.

| | |
|---|---|
| **SERVES 2** | 1 teaspoon Worcestershire sauce |
| 350 g (12 oz) potatoes, cut in | ¼ teaspoon English mustard |
| 1 cm (½ in) cubes | 2 x 100 g (4 oz) fillet steaks |
| 40 g (1½ oz) butter | 225 g (8 oz) spinach, washed |
| 1 tablespoon sunflower oil | and stalks removed |
| 1 onion, chopped | 1 tablespoon olive oil |
| 1½ teaspoon cornflour | 1 beefsteak tomato, chopped |
| 150 ml (¼ pint) red wine | 1 tablespoon mayonnaise |
| 250 ml (8 fl oz) beef stock | Salt and freshly ground black pepper |

Cook the potatoes in boiling, salted water for 10 minutes, until tender.

Heat 15 g (½ oz) of the butter and the sunflower oil in a frying-pan and cook the onion for 5 minutes, until golden. Put half of the fried onion in another pan, stir in the cornflour and cook for 2 minutes, stirring until golden. Gradually add the wine, stirring all the time. Add the stock, Worcestershire sauce, mustard and seasoning. Bring to the boil, stirring, and then leave to simmer for 10 minutes.

Season the steaks and cook them in a hot griddle pan for 6–8 minutes, turning once. Add the spinach to the remaining onion in the frying-pan and cook for 3 minutes, until wilted.

Heat the olive oil in a pan, add the tomato and cook for 2 minutes. Drain the potatoes and mash with the remaining butter, mayonnaise and salt and pepper. Stir in the chopped tomato.

To serve, pile the mashed potatoes on to serving plates, with the steak and spinach. Spoon the sauce around the steak.

## RICHARD CAWLEY

# SPOOKY SOUP WITH GORY GARNISH

### Pumpkin soup with sandwiches and ketchup

For this programme close to Hallowe'en, Richard made a treat for May Whitehead, from Oldham, who has a passion for ballroom dancing. May had brought a seasonal pumpkin with her, which Richard made into soup, accompanied by cheese and ham 'toasties'.

**SERVES 4**

**FOR THE SOUP**
700 g (1½ lb) pumpkin flesh, cut in 2 cm (¾ in) chunks
3 tablespoons soy sauce
2 tablespoons water
1 tablespoon sunflower oil
25 g (1 oz) butter
1 large onion, chopped
600 ml (1 pint) chicken or vegetable stock

**FOR THE SANDWICHES**
25 g (1 oz) butter
8 slices of bread
225 g (8 oz) Cheddar cheese, grated
100 g (4 oz) sliced ham
Salt and freshly ground black pepper
Sprigs of flatleaf parsley, to garnish
Tomato ketchup, to serve (optional)

Put the pumpkin in a microwave-proof bowl, with the soy sauce and water. Cover with cling film, pierce and cook in the microwave on full power for 5 minutes. Shake the bowl and cook on full power for another 3–5 minutes.

Heat the oil and butter in a large frying-pan, add the onion and cook for 8 minutes, until golden. Put two-thirds of the onion in a food processor with a third of the stock and whizz until finely chopped. Put the rest of the onion in a bowl and set it aside. Add the pumpkin and cooking liquid to the food processor, with the rest of the stock, season and whizz to a chunky soup.

Butter the slices of bread on one side and then, with the buttered side out, make four sandwiches with the grated cheese and ham.

Fry the sandwiches in batches in the frying-pan used to cook the onions, for 4–5 minutes, until golden, turning once. Alternatively, cook in a sandwich toaster. Cut each fried sandwich into quarters, garnish with sprigs of parsley and serve with tomato ketchup, if you like.

Ladle the pumpkin soup into bowls and scatter the rest of the onions over the top before serving.

## RICHARD CAWLEY

# ALISON'S SAUCY BARBECUE

Drumsticks and sausages with barbecue sauce and corn relish

According to the sons of Alison Sutherland, from Ipswich, Suffolk, her sausages are always a disaster on the barbecue and come out 'like black torpedoes'. Richard showed her how to cook sausages and chicken drumsticks on the barbecue or in the kitchen, with an easy barbecue sauce to accompany them.

**SERVES 2**
4 chicken drumsticks
6 sausages

**FOR THE BARBECUE SAUCE**
6 garlic cloves, 2 chopped, 4 sliced
2 tablespoons olive oil
2 tablespoons white wine vinegar
2 tablespoons white wine
2 tablespoons Worcestershire sauce
2 tablespoons tomato ketchup
Tabasco sauce
1/2 tablespoon water

**FOR THE CORN RELISH**
1 corn on the cob
1/2 onion, chopped
1 red pepper, seeded and chopped
2 teaspoons cornflour
2 tablespoons white wine vinegar
1/2 tablespoon water
2 teaspoons caster sugar
Salt and freshly ground black pepper

Pre-heat the oven to gas mark 6, 200°C (400°F). To make the barbecue sauce, sauté the chopped garlic in the oil for a minute.

Discard the garlic and add the vinegar, wine, Worcestershire sauce, tomato ketchup, a few drops of Tabasco and water to the pan. Bring the mixture to the boil and leave to simmer for 6 minutes, stirring occasionally.

Bake the drumsticks in the oven for 10 minutes. Then baste them with some of the barbecue sauce and return them to the oven. After 2–3 minutes, baste the chicken once again, turn, and cook it for a further 8–10 minutes.

Prick the sausages with a fork. Widen some of the pricks and stuff them with the sliced garlic. Then dry-fry or char-grill the sausages for 10–15 minutes, turning frequently.

To make the corn relish, remove the corn kernels from the cob by slicing down it with a knife. Cook the onion and red pepper in a tablespoon of water for 3 minutes. Add the corn and continue to cook for 2 minutes. In a cup, mix together the cornflour, vinegar and water and then stir into the corn. Add the sugar, season with salt and pepper and bring the mixture to the boil, stirring continuously. Let the sauce simmer until it thickens.

To serve, arrange the chicken and sausages on a plate. Serve the barbecue sauce and corn relish as accompaniments.

---

### READY STEADY COOK Tips

• *This easy barbecue sauce and the corn relish would also be excellent accompaniments to other barbecued food, such as pork chops or burgers.*

• *'Black torpedo' barbecue disasters are mostly caused by having the barbecue too hot, with too much charcoal. This can also lead to flare-ups and the danger that the inside of the food will be undercooked, even when the outside is inedibly charred.*

---

## RICHARD CAWLEY

# BARBARA'S BLACK-BEAN BEEF

Barbara May, from Liverpool, said that her rice always ended up a stodgy mess! Richard showed her how to make perfect rice to accompany a delicious beef stir-fry.

**SERVES 2**

**FOR THE FRIED RICE**
100 g (4 oz) basmati rice
1 tablespoon sunflower oil
6 spring onions, topped and tailed and sliced on the angle
2–3 tablespoons soy sauce

**FOR THE BEEF**
2 tablespoons sunflower oil
225 g (8 oz) frying steak, thinly sliced in long strips
1 garlic clove, chopped

1 red pepper, seeded and cut in 1 cm (½ in) squares
2.5 cm (1 in) root ginger, peeled and thinly sliced
½ cucumber, halved lengthways, seeded and cut in half-moons
160 g (5 ½ oz) jar black-bean sauce

**FOR THE GARNISH**
1 egg
1 tablespoon soy sauce
1 tablespoon sunflower oil
2 tablespoons chopped fresh coriander
Salt and freshly ground black pepper

Cook the rice according to the instructions on the packet. Drain it. Heat the oil in a large frying-pan and stir-fry the rice with 3 spring onions and 2–3 tablespoons of soy sauce for 2–3 minutes. At the end, add the chopped coriander.

For the beef stir-fry, heat the sunflower oil until very hot. Add the beef and cook for 2 minutes. Stir in the red pepper, garlic, ginger, cucumber, the remaining spring onions and black-bean sauce. Cook for 4–5 minutes.

To make the omelette, beat together the egg, a tablespoon of soy sauce and seasoning. Heat a tablespoon of oil in a small frying-pan and cook the omelette. Roll up the cooked omelette and slice it finely.

To serve, spoon the fried rice into the centre of a platter. Arrange half the beef on each side of the rice and sprinkle the omelette strips on top of the rice.

## R I C H A R D   C A W L E Y

# SPICY SAUSAGE AND MASH

Dawn Richardson came all the way from Cumbria to take part in the programme, bringing with her a locally made Cumberland sausage. Richard used it to make a warming winter recipe, combining it with parsnip and apple mash and a mushroom sauce.

**SERVES 2**

1 large Cumberland sausage, weighing about 500 g (1 lb)
100 g (4 oz) butter
1 potato, peeled and cubed small
1 garlic clove, chopped
1 tablespoon chopped fresh parsley
3 small parsnips, peeled and cut in small chunks

2 Cox's apples, peeled and cubed
Salt and freshly ground black pepper

**FOR THE SAUCE**
$\frac{1}{4}$ onion, finely chopped
1 tablespoon olive oil
50 g (2 oz) mushrooms, finely chopped
150 ml (5 fl oz) double cream
1 tablespoon Dijon mustard

Grill the Cumberland sausage for 18–20 minutes under a moderate grill, turning once. Clarify the butter by melting it over a gentle heat in a small pan, spooning off any white foam which comes to the surface. Then carefully pour off the clear golden liquid, leaving any sediment at the bottom of the pan.

Fry the potato in 2–3 tablespoons of clarified butter on a medium heat. Stir frequently to ensure even browning. When the potatoes are golden brown, stir in the garlic and parsley and cook for 3–4 minutes.

Meanwhile, boil the parsnips until they are almost cooked. Add the apple and cook until both are soft. Drain the parsnips and apple and then mash them with a little clarified butter and season the mixture.

For the sauce, fry the onion in the oil. When it begins to brown, add the mushrooms and cook for 3 minutes. Stir in the cream and mustard and bring to the boil. Turn down the heat and leave to simmer until the sauce has reduced by half.

To serve, make a bed of the mashed parsnips and apples, place the sausage on top and arrange the potatoes around the edge. Pour the sauce over and around the sausage.

## RICHARD CAWLEY

# PORKY THE FUNGI

### Pork chops with mushroom and mustard sauce and mashed swede

A self-styled 'domestic goddess' to her husband and two children, Soo Sherratt, from Shropshire, brought along some of her family's favourite pork and mushrooms to be turned into something 'divine' by Richard.

| SERVES 2 | |
| --- | --- |
| 1 medium swede, peeled and cubed | 1 onion, chopped |
| 2 tablespoons olive oil | 2 teaspoons dried sage |
| 2 x 150 g (6 oz) pork chops | 1 tablespoon chopped fresh parsley |
| 50 g (2 oz) mushrooms, sliced | 2 small Cox's apples, peeled and cubed |
| 85 ml (3 fl oz) double cream | 1 tablespoon Greek yoghurt |
| 1 teaspoon Dijon mustard | 1 teaspoon garam masala |
| | Salt and freshly ground black pepper |

Bring a pan of water to the boil, add the swede and leave it to cook for 15 minutes, until soft.

Meanwhile, heat a tablespoon of oil in a frying-pan. Season the chops with salt and pepper and fry them for about 6 minutes on each side over a moderate heat. Add the mushrooms half-way through cooking and stir in the cream and mustard for the last 2–3 minutes.

In a separate saucepan, heat a tablespoon of oil and fry the onion until soft. Add the sage, parsley, a spoonful of the cooked swede and the apples and cook for a further 5 minutes.

Drain the swede, return to the pan and mash it over the heat. Stir in the yoghurt and garam masala.

To serve, place a chop in the centre of a plate, pour over some of the mushroom and cream sauce and surround with the mashed swede and apple mixture.

## PATRICK ANTHONY

# PORK AND CIDER WITH ROS

### Pork slices, with cider and mushroom sauce and sweet-and-sour marrow

West Country specialities – pork and cider – were the ingredients chosen by Rosalind Sims from Bristol. Patrick transformed them into a delicious dish of pork and mushrooms in a cream, cider and tarragon sauce, accompanied by spicy marrow.

**SERVES 2**

**FOR THE MARROW**
½ small marrow, peeled, seeded and cubed
2 tomatoes
1 tablespoon tomato purée
1 teaspoon sugar
4 drops of Tabasco sauce
2 teaspoons red wine vinegar
A pinch of ground coriander
½ teaspoon Dijon mustard

**FOR THE PORK**
225 g (8 oz) pork tenderloin, sliced thinly
2 tablespoons plain flour, seasoned
3 tablespoons olive oil
1 onion, chopped
1 apple, cored and chopped
75 ml (3 fl oz) cider
100 g (4 oz) button mushrooms, quartered
2–3 tablespoons double cream
2 teaspoons chopped fresh tarragon
5 drops of Worcestershire sauce
Salt and freshly ground black pepper

Boil the marrow chunks in a shallow pan in a little water for 3–5 minutes. Drain and return to the pan. Add the tomatoes, tomato purée, sugar, Tabasco, vinegar, coriander and mustard. Leave to simmer for 15 minutes, stirring occasionally.

Season the pork slices, coat them with a little flour and fry them in 2 tablespoons of oil for 5–7 minutes, turning half-way. Set aside.

Sauté the onion and apple in the remaining oil for 3 minutes. Add the cider and mushrooms. Season and cook for 5 minutes, stirring occasionally. Add the pork and stir in the cream, tarragon and Worcestershire sauce. Leave to simmer for 10 minutes.

To serve, spoon the pork and mushrooms into the centre of the plates. Surround with the marrow.

## PATRICK ANTHONY

# BARBARA'S BUMPER BEEF

### Steak in a creamy mushroom sauce, with pasta

Barbara Epstein, from the Wirral, Merseyside, is proud of her three children, two grandchildren and a 'bumper' appetite. Some of her favourite foods appear in Patrick's recipe for steak strips in a creamy mushroom sauce, on a bed of pasta.

| | |
|---|---|
| **SERVES 2** | 1 garlic clove, chopped |
| 150 g (6 oz) pappardelle (broad ribbon pasta) | 1 teaspoon Dijon mustard |
| or tagliatelle | Finely chopped fresh parsley |
| 225 g (8 oz) rump steak | Worcestershire sauce |
| 25 g (1 oz) butter | 75 ml (3 fl oz) white wine |
| 1 tablespoon oil | 100 g (4 oz) mushrooms, sliced |
| ½ onion, finely chopped | 4 tablespoons double cream |
| 1 red pepper, seeded and diced | ½ Savoy cabbage, finely shredded |
| 1 green pepper, seeded and diced | |

Cook the pasta, according to the directions on the packet.

Pat the rump steak dry with kitchen paper and cut it in thin strips. Put a knob of butter in a frying-pan, with a dash of oil (this prevents the butter from burning). Add the steak and chopped onion and cook until brown. Remove the steak and place on one side.

In the same pan, add the peppers, garlic, mustard, parsley, a splash of Worcestershire sauce and the wine. Allow to boil furiously, to remove the alcohol. Add the mushrooms and return the cooked steak; then add the double cream and season.

Quickly blanch the cabbage in a little boiling, salted water. Pour the sauce on to the pasta and serve with the cabbage.

PATRICK  ANTHONY

# DEBBIE'S DELIGHT

Pasta with beef patties and tomato sauce, and leeks
with gold-medal sauce

Although traditional Welsh recipes such as Welsh broth and Welshcakes were the staples of Deborah Stoddart's Merthyr Tydfil childhood, these days she prefers Mediterranean-style meals. Some of her favourite ingredients, bought for the occasion, go into Patrick's dish; the gold-medal sauce is so named because its versatility and ease of preparation make it a winner.

**SERVES 2**

300 ml (10 fl oz) passata
A pinch of sugar

**FOR THE PATTIES**

1 tablespoon chopped fresh parsley

225 g (8 oz) lean minced beef
1 egg
Worcestershire sauce
1 teaspoon dried oregano
2 tablespoons olive oil

**FOR THE LEEKS IN GOLD-MEDAL SAUCE**

1 leek, halved and cut in half again lengthways
2 egg yolks
1 teaspoon French mustard
1 teaspoon white wine vinegar
100 g (4 oz) butter

**FOR THE PASTA AND TOMATO SAUCE**

225 g (8 oz) lasagnette or tagliatelle
1 tablespoon olive oil
1/4 onion, finely chopped

1 tablespoon fresh herbs (parsley, chives, chervil), freshly chopped (optional)
Salt and freshly ground black pepper

Put the minced beef into a bowl, add an egg, a dash of
Worcestershire sauce and oregano and season with salt and pepper.
Work the ingredients together with a fork. Form into small patties on a
floured board. Heat the oil and fry the patties on both sides, until
lightly browned. Remove, drain and keep warm.

Cook the pasta, following the instructions on the packet.

Heat the remaining oil in a frying-pan, add the onion and fry it until
softened. Add the passata and a pinch of salt and sugar and cook
until reduced to a thick sauce.

Cook the leeks for 3 minutes in boiling salted water, until just soft.

For the gold-medal sauce, put the egg yolks in a bowl, beat in the
mustard and vinegar and season with salt and pepper. Melt the butter,
but don't let it get too hot as the eggs may scramble, and whisk it into
the egg-yolk mixture. Add the herbs, if using. If you wish to thicken the
sauce, set the bowl over a pan of simmering water and whisk it.
Avoid adding the white residue from the butter if you can.

To serve, drain the pasta, divide it between two serving plates and
pile the meat patties on top. Cover with the tomato sauce and sprinkle
with parsley. Drain the leeks, place on the plate and cover with the
gold-medal sauce.

---

### READY STEADY COOK Tip

*• The method for making the gold-medal sauce is similar to
making hollandaise sauce or mayonnaise. The trick is not to add
the melted butter too fast and also to make sure that the sauce
doesn't get too hot, otherwise the yolks will become grainy.*

## PATRICK ANTHONY

# CLAIRE'S TURKISH CREATION

Lamb steaks with pilaff and creamy beans

Claire Jones, from Cardiff, loves Turkish food. She brought along some characteristically Turkish ingredients – including lamb and dried apricots – and asked Patrick to turn them into a Turkish-style treat. Patrick obliged with this sophisticated version of a pilaff, seared lamb steaks and creamy beans.

**SERVES 2**

**FOR THE PILAFF**
1 tablespoon sunflower oil
15 g (½ oz) butter
1 onion, chopped
100 g (4 oz) long-grain rice
300 ml (10 fl oz) chicken stock
50 g (2 oz) no-soak dried apricots, finely chopped

**FOR THE BEANS**
150 g (6 oz) runner beans, cut in 2 cm (¾ in) lengths

75 ml (3 fl oz) white wine
150 ml (¼ pint) double cream
2 tablespoons chopped fresh tarragon

**FOR THE LAMB**
Olive oil
2 x 100 g (4 oz) boneless lamb leg steaks
Tabasco sauce
Salt and freshly ground black pepper
Chopped fresh mint and sprigs of flatleaf parsley, to garnish

Heat a tablespoon of oil and the butter in a pan, add half of the onion and cook for 2 minutes. Stir in the rice, until coated in oil, and then add the stock, apricots and seasoning. Cover and leave to simmer for 10 minutes, or until all the liquid has been absorbed and the rice is tender.

Cook the runner beans in boiling water for 3 minutes. Drain and refresh them under cold running water. Put the wine and the rest of the chopped onion in a pan and simmer for 3 minutes. Add the cream, tarragon and seasoning and simmer for 3 minutes. Stir in the runner beans and cook for 2 minutes.

Rub a little olive oil and seasoning into the lamb steaks and cook them in a pre-heated griddle pan or heavy-based frying-pan over a moderately high heat for 4 minutes, turning once. Sprinkle over a few drops of Tabasco sauce.

Spoon the rice into two ramekin dishes, press down, and then turn out on to two serving plates. Sprinkle the chopped mint on top of the rice. Place the lamb steaks and creamy beans around the rice and garnish with sprigs of flatleaf parsley.

## PATRICK ANTHONY

# SARAH'S STEAK SENSATION

### Coconut beef curry, with rice and courgettes

Currying steak is an unusual and delicious idea. Sarah Witts, from Welwyn Garden City, Hertfordshire, brought rump steak and Eastern spices, in the hope that Patrick could make a curry delicious enough to tempt her husband, Anthony, to be more adventurous in what he eats.

**SERVES 2**

100 g (4 oz) long-grain rice

150 ml (5 fl oz) double cream
50 g (2 oz) creamed coconut
Salt and freshly ground black pepper

**FOR THE CURRY**

1 tablespoon sunflower oil
1 onion, chopped
1 garlic clove, finely chopped
1 teaspoon ginger purée
2 teaspoons medium-hot curry powder
4 tablespoons water
350 g (12 oz) rump steak, batted with a rolling pin to tenderize, and cut in thin strips

**FOR THE COURGETTES**

15 g (½ oz) butter
2 courgettes, grated
1 fresh red chilli, seeded and finely chopped
1 teaspoon soy sauce
Juice of ½ a lime
Finely chopped red pepper and sprigs of coriander, to garnish

Cook the rice in boiling water for 10–12 minutes, until tender.

Heat the oil in a frying-pan, add the onion and cook for 2 minutes. Stir in the garlic, ginger purée and curry powder and cook for a minute. Add 4 tablespoons of water and cook for 2 minutes. Stir in the strips of beef and seasoning and stir-fry for 3 minutes. Add the cream and simmer for 3 minutes.

Melt the butter in a frying-pan, add the courgettes, chilli and seasoning and stir-fry for 3 minutes. Add the soy sauce and lime juice.

Grate the creamed coconut into the beef curry. Cook for 2 minutes, stirring, until the creamed coconut has melted and the sauce has thickened slightly.

Drain the rice well, spoon it into a ramekin dish, press it down and then turn it out on to a serving plate. Spoon the beef curry and courgettes around the rice. Scatter a little red pepper on top of the rice and garnish the curry with sprigs of coriander.

---

### READY STEADY COOK Tips

• Creamed coconut adds a delicious creamy texture to dishes as well as the delicious coconut flavour. It dissolves very quickly if you grate it and it's a really good way to thicken the sauces of all kinds of curries and casseroles, if you don't want to use cornflour.

• Using strips of tender, lean meat like steak is a good way of speeding up the cooking times of curries; combined with stir-frying techniques, you can rustle up an oriental feast in minutes.

## PATRICK ANTHONY

# TRACY'S BARBIE BONANZA

### Lamb burgers and meatballs

Minced meat is wonderful for creating unusual ideas for barbecues and because it goes a long way, it is very economical. Tracy Wordley, from Sudbury, Suffolk, had brought both minced lamb and minced beef, which Patrick used for two tasty summer barbecue dishes.

**SERVES 4**

1 red pepper, seeded and cut in 3–4 pieces
2 teaspoons white wine vinegar
2 teaspoons honey
Tabasco sauce
2 onions, chopped
2 tablespoons chopped mixed fresh dill, basil and chervil
2 courgettes, grated
½ tablespoon sunflower oil
Olive oil
1 garlic clove (optional)
Salt and freshly ground black pepper

**FOR THE LAMB BURGERS**

1 French stick
450 g (1 lb) minced lamb
1 egg, beaten
1 teaspoon dried oregano
½ tablespoon sunflower oil

**FOR THE MEATBALLS**

225 g (8 oz) minced beef
1 egg, beaten
Tabasco sauce
1 teaspoon garam masala
A pinch of hot madras curry powder
½ teaspoon wholegrain mustard
1–2 tablespoons plain flour

To make the lamb burgers, use enough white crumb from the baguette to give 2 tablespoons of breadcrumbs. Mix together the minced lamb, breadcrumbs and egg and season with salt, pepper and oregano. Then shape the mixture into four burgers and char-grill them, brushed with sunflower oil, for 3–4 minutes on each side, or longer for well-done burgers.

For the meatballs, mix together the minced beef, part of an egg, 4 drops of Tabasco, the garam masala, curry powder, mustard and enough flour to make a fairly stiff mixture. Form the mixture into small balls and char-grill them for 5–7 minutes. Once the meatballs are cooked, thread them on to kebab sticks.

Place the pieces of pepper under a hot grill until the skin blisters and blackens. Put the peppers into a polythene bag and knot the end. Leave until cool enough to handle and then peel off the skin.

Heat the vinegar, honey and 3 drops of Tabasco in a saucepan. Add the onions and cook until they are caramelized. Add the fresh herbs and continue to cook for a few minutes.

Season the grated courgettes and sauté them in the remaining sunflower oil.

Cut two 5 cm (2 in) thick long diagonal slices from the baguette. Drizzle a little olive oil and rub a cut clove of garlic, if liked, over both sides and toast under a grill. The remaining bread can be used to accompany the meal.

To serve, place each lamb burger on top of a piece of toasted bread and arrange them on a platter, with the meatballs and red pepper. Surround with the onion and courgettes.

---

### READY STEADY COOK Tip

• *If you're not barbecuing, serve the lamb burger with burgerbuns and salad for a main course. Try the meatballs with tomato sauce and pasta shapes.*

---

# DESSERTS

## PATRICK ANTHONY

# CAROL'S CHRISTMAS FANTASY

Sponge casing filled with flambéed dates and banana, with a creamy, lemony yoghurt topping

Containing a medley of Christmas flavours – chestnut, nuts and dried fruit, brandy and orange – this is an exciting, lighter alternative to Christmas Pudding. Carol Markellow, from South London, wanted Patrick to show her a festive but different idea to finish off her family's Christmas dinner and Patrick obliged with this fantastical Christmas creation.

**SERVES 4–6**

2 tablespoons unsweetened chestnut purée
250 ml (8 fl oz) double cream
6 tablespoons caster sugar
2 tablespoons chopped, mixed nuts
½ lemon, heated in a little hot water
250 ml (8 fl oz) Greek yoghurt
15 g (½ oz) butter

1 banana, sliced
6 fresh dates, stoned and quartered
A splash of brandy
6 slices of marble cake, ½ inch thick
2 satsumas, peeled and segmented
A few sprigs of fresh mint
1 orange, peeled and sliced
1 teaspoon icing sugar

To make the chestnut cream, stir together the purée, 175 ml (6 fl oz) of the cream and a tablespoon of sugar over a low heat for 4–5 minutes until the sugar has dissolved and the mixture is smooth. Sprinkle the nuts into a dry frying-pan and heat until browned, stirring often.

In a bowl, mix together 3 tablespoons of caster sugar, the juice from the half lemon, the yoghurt and the remaining double cream. Melt the butter in a frying-pan, add the remaining caster sugar, the banana and dates. When the pan is very hot, pour in a splash of brandy. Set light to the brandy to flambé the fruit. Line a bowl with slices of the cake. Spoon in the date and banana mixture, add the chestnut cream and then put a layer of satsuma segments on top. Finally, pour over the yoghurt and cream mixture and sprinkle with the nuts. Garnish with the mint and orange slices and sprinkle with icing sugar.

## PATRICK ANTHONY

# CAROLYN'S FRUIT BASKET CREATION

These brandy-snap baskets with caramelized fruit served with chocolate sauce are an excellent dessert that look beautiful but take only a few minutes to do. That makes it ideal for Carolyn Hall, from Tyne and Wear, a busy young mum who is usually too busy to cook, let alone entertain.

**SERVES 2**

**FOR THE CHOCOLATE SAUCE**
75 g (3 oz) plain chocolate
85 ml (3 fl oz) warm water
3 tablespoons double cream
50 g (2 oz) butter

**FOR THE FRUIT BASKETS**
A little lemon juice
2 small pears, cored and chopped

2 small apples, cored and chopped
4 brandy snaps
15 g (½ oz) almond flakes
50 g (2 oz) butter
35 g (1½ oz) caster sugar
1 teaspoon ground cinnamon
A little shredded zest of orange
A little shredded zest of lime
A little shredded zest of lemon
Fresh mint leaves, to garnish

Pre-heat the oven to gas mark 6, 200°C (400°F). Squeeze a little lemon juice over the apple and pear flesh, to prevent it from discolouring. Melt the chocolate with 85 ml (3 fl oz) of water. When the chocolate has melted, stir in the cream and cook for 2–3 minutes. Then add the butter.

Lay a piece of baking parchment or greaseproof paper on a baking tray. Place the brandy snaps and the almond flakes on this and bake in the oven for 1–2 minutes, until the brandy snaps are flat and malleable. Leave the almonds in the oven for 5 minutes longer, until they are toasted golden brown. Place the brandy snaps over upturned cups to form baskets; then leave to harden.

Caramelize the apples and pears in the remaining butter and the caster sugar. After 4 minutes, add the cinnamon and continue to cook until the fruit has turned golden.

To serve, make a lake of chocolate sauce on two plates. Arrange two brandy-snap baskets on top on each plate. Fill each basket with the caramelized fruit and toasted almonds, and garnish with the citrus fruit zest and some fresh mint leaves.

## P A T R I C K   A N T H O N Y

# JOANNE'S PANCAKE JOY

### Fruit-filled pancakes with raspberry-wine sauce

Sweet-toothed Joanne Wall, from Bristol, had brought some of her own home-made wine and favourite fruit and Patrick transformed them into a Shrove Tuesday celebration pudding of pancakes filled with blueberries, strawberries and pecans in an orange liqueur and raspberry-wine sauce.

**SERVES 4**

**FOR THE PANCAKES**
50 g (2 oz) plain flour
1 egg
100 ml (3½ fl oz) milk
100 ml (3½ fl oz) water
25 g (1 oz) butter, melted
Sunflower oil, for frying

**FOR THE FILLING**
25 g (1 oz) butter
25 g (1 oz) caster sugar
Juice of 1–2 oranges
50 ml (2 fl oz) raspberry wine (optional)
50 g (2 oz) dried blueberries or prunes, or raisins
8 pecan halves, chopped
1 tablespoon orange liqueur
150 g (6 oz) punnet of strawberries, hulled and halved or quartered if large
150 ml (5 fl oz) double cream, to serve

To make the pancake batter, sieve the flour into a mixing bowl, make a well in it and break 2 eggs into the well. Whisk the eggs and flour together, add the milk and water gradually and continue to whisk until smooth. Slowly add the melted butter.

83

To make light, thin crêpes, heat a little oil in a pan. When it is very hot add 2 tablespoons of the batter and swirl it to cover the bottom of the pan. Patch up any holes with more batter. Cook until underside is golden. Flip over and brown second side. Repeat to make three more pancakes.

For the pancake filling, melt the butter and mix in the sugar and the orange juice (use half if using raspberry wine). Stir with a wooden spoon and cook for 3 minutes. Add the raspberry wine, if using, the blueberries and pecans and cook for a further 6–8 minutes. Stir in the liqueur and strawberries and continue to cook for 3 minutes.

Put 2 tablespoons of the sauce on each cooked pancake and fold the pancake. To serve, pour the cream on to a plate and put the filled pancakes on top. Pour the rest of the sauce around the pancakes.

## PATRICK ANTHONY

# VICKY'S PINEAPPLE VICTORY

*It's amazing what a variety of delicious ideas can be generated from one fresh pineapple! Looking forward to summer, Vicky Burns, from Macclesfield, had been on a diet and wanted to give herself a tropical treat.*

| SERVES 2 | 45 g (1¾ oz) butter |
|---|---|
| 1 medium pineapple, skin, spikes and core removed, flesh cut in 2.5 cm (1 in) thick rings | ½ teaspoon honey |
| | 3 eggs |
| 65 g (2½ oz) caster sugar | 5 tablespoons double cream |
| 50 ml (2 fl oz) rum | 75 g (3 oz) plain chocolate, melted |
| 225 g (8 oz) punnet of strawberries | 175 ml (6 fl oz) milk |
| 200 g (7 oz) Greek yoghurt | 2–3 fresh mint leaves, to garnish |
| 2 tablespoons icing sugar | Ice cubes, to serve |

For the pineapple kebabs, cut a pineapple ring into eight pieces and thread them on to three wooden skewers. Coat the fruit in caster sugar and fry in a dry pan for 2 minutes, until caramelized on each side. Flambé the pineapple by adding 3 teaspoons of the rum and setting it alight.

For the yoghurt sauce, mash two strawberries into 2 tablespoons of yoghurt. Mix thoroughly. Hull and cut three strawberries in half lengthways.

To serve, arrange the pineapple kebabs on a plate, placing a strawberry half on the ends of each kebab. Spoon the yoghurt sauce on the side as a dip.

For the caramelized pineapple ring, coat a pineapple ring in icing sugar and fry in 15 g (½ oz) of butter in a hot pan for 3–4 minutes on each side.

For the rum sauce, mix the remaining rum with the honey and heat gently for 5 minutes.

To make the sweet omelette, whisk together the eggs, 15 g (½ oz) of caster sugar and 2 tablespoons of the double cream. Fry in 15 g (½ oz) of butter for 2–3 minutes on one side only, folding it over to make an omelette.

To serve, arrange the fried pineapple ring, pour over the rum sauce and then place the sweet omelette on top and sprinkle it with icing sugar.

For the pineapple with chocolate sauce, chop the remaining fresh pineapple into cubes. Melt the chocolate with the remaining butter, to make a glossy sauce. To serve, arrange the pineapple cubes on a lake of cream, pour over the chocolate sauce.

For the strawberry milkshake, mix together the milk, remaining yoghurt, a tablespoon of icing sugar and 6 strawberries in a liquidizer. To serve, pour into two tall glasses with a few ice cubes and decorate with strawberries and mint leaves.

## RICHARD CAWLEY

# YUMMY SCRUMMY FLYING SAUCER

### Steamed pudding with caramel sauce

Justine Hammond, from Nottingham, had brought the ingredients for a classic old-fashioned steamed pudding. Justine loves to experiment with new dishes but she said she wasn't too confident with traditional English cooking. Richard showed her this classic steamed pudding, served with a caramel cream sauce, which is made in minutes in the microwave.

**SERVES 4**

100 g (4 oz) self-raising flour
50 g (2 oz) caster sugar
50 g (2 oz) butter, softened
1 egg
4 tablespoons milk
225 g (8 oz) fresh dates, stoned
2 tablespoons flaked coconut

Grated zest of 1 lemon
1 satsuma, peeled and sliced
1 tablespoon clear honey

**FOR THE SAUCE**

5 tablespoons caster sugar
1 tablespoon water
150 ml (5 fl oz) double cream

Butter a microwave-proof 900 ml (1½ pint) pudding basin or bowl. Put the flour, sugar, butter and egg in a food processor and whizz until the mixture looks like fine breadcrumbs. With the motor still running, gradually add the milk and whizz until the mixture is smooth. Chop half of the dates and stir them into the pudding mixture, with the flaked coconut and lemon zest.

Line the sides of the pudding basin with the satsuma slices and spoon the honey into the base. Carefully spoon the pudding mixture into the basin. Cook in the microwave on high power for 4½ minutes. Leave to rest for 5 minutes.

Meanwhile, gently heat the caster sugar in a small pan. Add the water and continue to cook gently until the sugar has dissolved. Simmer for 2–3 minutes, until the syrup turns to a golden caramel.

Push whole dates on to the ends of four wooden skewers and then dip them in the caramel. Put on a sheet of baking parchment or greaseproof paper and leave to set.

Stir the cream into the rest of the caramel and let it simmer for 2 minutes. Turn the pudding out on to a serving plate, pour the cream sauce around the base of the pudding and decorate with the caramel-coated dates.

## R I C H A R D   C A W L E Y

# KATE AND RICHARD'S SAUCY TARTS

Apricot and plum tartlets, with fruit brûlée

Kate Wilkinson and her husband Richard, from Warwickshire, were looking forward to celebrating their wedding anniversary and Richard's birthday the following day. Richard Cawley made this easy triple dessert of two different kinds of fruit tart and a fruit brûlée to put them in the right mood.

| | |
|---|---|
| **SERVES 2** | 8–10 plums, stoned and quartered |
| 100 g (4 oz) puff pastry | 120 ml (4 fl oz) red wine |
| 1 egg yolk, beaten | 50 g (2 oz) brown sugar |
| 8–10 apricots, stoned and quartered | ¼ teaspoon ground cinnamon |
| 120 ml (4 fl oz) white wine | ¼ teaspoon ground ginger |
| 100 g (4 oz) caster sugar | A few mint leaves, chopped |
| Seeds from 3 cardamom pods | 200 g (7 oz) tub Greek yoghurt |

Pre-heat the oven to gas mark 7, 220°C (425°F).

Roll out the pastry until it is 3–5 mm (⅛–¼ in) thick. Brush with the egg yolk and then cut out four 4-inch rounds with a pastry cutter. Bake the pastry circles on the middle shelf of an oven for 8–10 minutes. Allow the pastry circles to cool and then slice each one horizontally.

Meanwhile, for the apricot compote, heat half the apricots in a pan with the white wine, 75 g (3 oz) of the caster sugar and the cardamom seeds. Bring to the boil and then let the apricots simmer for 10 minutes, until the mixture is thick and jammy.

To make the plum compote, in a separate pan, heat two or three of the plums with the red wine, brown sugar, cinnamon and ginger. Bring to the boil and simmer for 10 minutes, until the mixture is thick and jammy, like the apricot compote.

Spoon the apricot compote on to two pastry halves and the plum compote on to another two and then cover each with a pastry lid.

For the fruit brûlée, roughly chop the remaining apricot and plum quarters and put them in two ramekins, with the chopped mint. Pour over the yoghurt, and then sprinkle over the remaining sugar. Place under a very hot grill and leave until the sugar has caramelized.

To serve, arrange one of each pastries on a plate with the fruit brûlée.

## RICHARD CAWLEY

# EASTER STRAWBERRY NESTS

**A sweet tooth and a passion for puddings were amongst the ingredients that Jayne Robertson, from Essex, brought along to a programme broadcast near Easter. Richard made her this springtime treat of puff pastry nests filled with strawberries and cherries and served with caramel sauce.**

|  |  |
|---|---|
| **SERVES 2** | 120 ml (4 fl oz) double cream |
| 1 packet of ready-rolled puff pastry | 75 g (3 oz) dried cherries, chopped |
| 1 egg yolk | 10 strawberries, halved |
| 1 tablespoon milk | 25 g (1 oz) butter |
| 250 g (9 oz) caster sugar | 25 g (1 oz) walnuts, chopped |
| 1 tablespoon water | |

Pre-heat the oven to gas mark 6, 200°C (400°F).For the pastry nests, cut the thawed pastry into two 20 cm (8 in) squares. Mix the egg yolk and milk to make a glaze and brush the squares with this. Using a sharp knife, make cuts 2.5 cm (1 in) from the edges, stopping 3 cm (1 1/4 in) short at two opposing corners (see diagam 1 below). Bring one cut edge over and place along the opposite inside corner of the square and then repeat with the other cut edge (see diagrams 2 and 3). Brush the basket again with the egg and milk mixture. Repeat with the other pastry square and bake in the oven for 15 minutes.

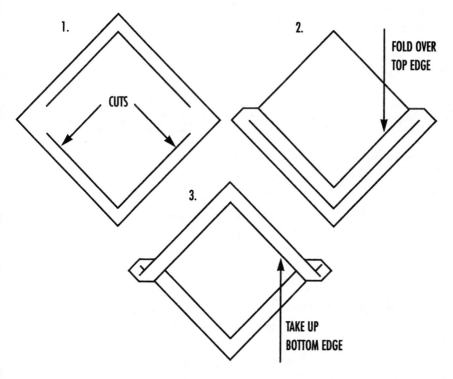

To make sugar shards, place a sheet of foil on a baking sheet. Spread 150 g (5 oz) of caster sugar on the foil and place under a hot grill until the sugar has turned brown, liquid and completely transparent. Check the sugar regularly, as it burns easily. Remove from the grill and allow to cool and harden and then break into jagged pieces of varying sizes.

To make the caramel sauce, dissolve 75 g (3 oz) of sugar in water over a gentle heat. When the sugar begins to caramelize, pour in the double cream, stirring continuously. Any lumps that appear when the cream is added will quickly dissolve. Add half of the chopped cherries.

Sauté the strawberries and the remaining cherries with the butter and the remaining sugar for 2–3 minutes.

To serve, arrange each pastry nest on a plate. Spoon the strawberries into the pastry nest and pour the caramel sauce around the pastry. Garnish with the chopped walnuts and the sugar shards.

## RICHARD CAWLEY

# DR CLARK'S GINGER PUD

*Believing that her dinner-party desserts let her down, Melanie Chown, from West London, hoped* Ready Steady Cook *would provide the answer. Richard saved the day with his simple, frothy syllabub, served with ginger-stuffed lychees, pink grapefruit segments and home-made ginger biscuits. Named after Richard's parents' doctor, who was passionate about these ginger biscuits, this dish will work like a dream.*

**SERVES 2**
400 g (14 oz) tin of lychees
6 whole pieces of stem ginger in syrup, quartered

**FOR THE BISCUITS**
100 g (4 oz) golden syrup
75 g (3 oz) butter
1 egg
225 g (8 oz) self-raising flour
1 heaped teaspoon ground ginger
A pinch of salt

**TO SERVE**
150 ml (5 fl oz) double cream
2 teaspoons caster sugar
1 tablespoon grapefruit juice
3 tablespoons Muscat or other sweet wine
1 meringue nest, crumbled
$\frac{1}{2}$ pink grapefruit, cut into segments

Pre-heat the oven to gas mark 6, 200°C (400°F). Drain the lychees from their syrup and stuff them with some of the pieces of ginger.

For the biscuits, pour the golden syrup into a food processor, add the butter and egg and blend everything together. Then add the flour, ginger and a pinch of salt and blend again. Put a teaspoonful of mixture for each biscuit on to a greased baking tray (this quantity should make 24 biscuits) and bake in the pre-heated oven for 5–6 minutes, until golden brown.

Whip together the double cream, sugar, grapefruit juice and a tablespoon of wine, until thickened. Fold in the crumbled meringue. Chop a few more pieces of stem ginger and fold them into the cream.

To serve, put four or five stuffed lychees into two tall, stemmed glasses, pour over a tablespoon of wine and spoon half the whipped-cream mixture into each. Decorate two plates with alternate segments of grapefruit, stuffed lychees and ginger biscuits around the edge and put the glasses in the centre of the plates.

---

### READY STEADY COOK Tip

• *With the lychees and ginger, this dessert would be an ideal finale to an oriental-style dinner party, while being creamy and delicious enough to satisfy the greediest dessert-lover.*

---

# INDEX

## A

apples,
    sausage and mash 69–70
apricot and plum tartlets, with fruit
    brûlée 87–8
artichoke crisps 19–20
aubergines
    filo pastry boats with two
        vegetable fillings 17–18
    sautéed with stuffed mushrooms
        and cheese sauce 20–1
avocado and chicory salad 22

## B

barbecue sauce and corn relish with
    drumsticks and sausages 66–7
beans
    lamb steaks with pilaff and
        creamy beans 75–6
    Thai chicken curry, with lemon rice
        and sesame beans 46–7
    turkey chilli with tortillas, re-fried
        beans and yoghurt-chilli dip
        59–60
beef
    black-bean beef 68–9
    coconut beef curry with rice and
        courgettes 76–7
    meatballs 78–9
    pasta with beef patties and
        tomato sauce and leeks in
        gold-medal sauce 73–4
    steak in a creamy mushroom
        sauce with pasta 72–3

steak with red-wine sauce,
    mashed potatoes and
    spinach 64
beurre blanc sauce with turkey
    escalopes 41
bulghar wheat with fried chicken
    and tomato and orange
    salad 55–6
caramel sauce, steamed pudding
    with 86–7

## C

carrots
    carrot and orange salad 36–7
    carrot puffs 61–2
cauliflower and root vegetables in a
    creamy curry sauce 15–16
cheese
    cheese-topped chicken with salsify
        sauce 54
    rabbit with Stilton sauce and fried
        potatoes 58
    soufflés 22
chestnuts
    Christmas fantasy 81
    and cranberry pudding 12–13
chicken
    breadcrumbed with creamy pasta
        sauce 48–9
    cheese-topped with salsify
        sauce 54
    drumsticks with barbecue sauce
        and corn relish 66–7
    fried with bulghar wheat and
        tomato and orange salad 55–6
    in ginger and pineapple sauce
        44–5
    lemon 42–3

# INDEX

# INDEX